POINTS
OF
DEPARTURE

POINTS OF DEPARTURE

Zen Buddhism with a Rinzai View

EIDO T. SHIMANO

Copyright © 1991 by Eido T. Shimano

All rights reserved. No part of this book may be used or reproduced in any form without written permission from the publisher except in cases of brief quotations embodied in critical articles and reviews. For information, contact:
  The Zen Studies Society Press
  HCR1, Box 171
  Livingston Manor, New York 12758
  FAX 914-439-3119

German translation published by
Theseus-Verlag AG, Zürich, Switzerland

First Edition
1 2 3 4 5 6 7 8 9

Printed in the United States of America

Hardcover ISBN: 0-962946-1-X
Softcover ISBN: 0-962946-0-1

Eido T. Shimano

Eido T. Shimano is abbot of New York Zendo in New York City, and of Dai Bosatsu Zendo in upstate New York. He trained as a Rinzai Zen Buddhist monk under Gempo Roshi and Nakagawa Soen Roshi in Japan, and studied several years with Yasutani Roshi. He is an heir of Soen Roshi's lineage. Eido Roshi came to New York in 1960 and is now an American citizen, active in American Zen Buddhism and in Buddhist-Christian relations. *Points of Departure* is his latest book.

Editor's Note

Eido Roshi's previous book of teishos or Dharma talks, GOLDEN WIND, has been out of print for some time. Although Zen Buddhism itself is timeless, the ways of presenting its insights evolve in the culture, and the teacher's "vista" — one of Eido Roshi's favorite words — is always widening.

This book offers an emphasis on the Rinzai Zen tradition so that its special way of understanding Zen will not be lost to students in our rapidly changing society. It is meant only to enrich the study of Zen, not to partition it.

We have tried to offer this material in some developmental order:

first, a look at Zen Buddhist spirituality with its view of Buddha Nature, or Ultimate Reality, as expressed through Eido Roshi's experience;

next, a glimpse of some areas where change and spiritual growth may be occurring in the reader;

then, a taste of spiritual practice with a Rinzai flavor;

and finally, a sample of the way thought and practice fuse, as illustrated in several complete teishos.

I am grateful to Eido Roshi and to the DBZ Sangha, for the opportunity to work on, and in, and with this book.

Gassho,

Myoshin Lorette Zirker

•

Acknowledgments

The text of this book was prepared from tapes of Eido Roshi's teaching-talks (teishos) at Dai Bosatsu Zendo, Livingston Manor, New York and at New York Zendo in New York City. The tapes were directly and meticulously transcribed by Saman Lea Liu. They were then edited for the reader and reworked.

The edition of the *Rinzai Roku, The Record of Lin Chi*, most frequently used for the English translations of "the sayings and doings of Master Rinzai" was edited by Ruth F. Sasaki and published by the Institute for Zen Studies, Kyoto, and is quoted with permission.

The koan material in English is drawn from *Two Zen Classics: Mumonkan, the Gateless Gate, and Hekiganroku, the Blue Cliff Record* by Katsuki Sekida, published by John Weatherhill, Inc., New York.

The Book of Equanimity (Shoyo Roku) is not available in English. There is a partial translation in an unpublished manuscript of Nyogen Senzaki's.

The Iron Flute, One Hundred Zen Koan, was translated and edited by Nyogen Senzaki and Ruth Strout McCandless, and published by Charles E. Tuttle Company, Inc., Rutland, Vermont.

The quotation on the Man of Buji by D. T. Suzuki was taken from *The Awakening of Zen*, by D.T. Suzuki, copyright 1980 by The Buddhist Society. It is reprinted by arrangement with Shambhala Publications, Inc., 300 Massachusetts Avenue, Boston 02115.

Quotations from the Diamond Sutra are from a translation by A. F. Price, in *The Diamond Sutra and The Sutra of Hui Neng*, published by Shambhala Publications and adapted by Eido Roshi and his students.

Nyogen Senzaki's prayer is taken from *Like A Dream, Like A Fantasy*, a collection of Senzaki's writings translated and edited by Eido Roshi, published by Japan Publications, Tokyo.

Some of the material on koans has appeared in different form in "Koans", *Zen: Tradition and Transition*, edited by Kenneth Kraft and published by Grove Press, New York.

Namu Dai Bosa, A Transmission of Zen Buddhism to America, selections from the writings of Nyogen Senzaki, Nakagawa Soen Roshi, and Eido Roshi, was edited by Louis Nordstrom and published by Theatre Arts Books, New York.

Other phrases in quotation marks are taken from the Morning Service as it is recited at Dai Bosatsu Zendo, or from some of the often recited poems and chants used at the zendo. The texts for these may be found in the zendo's Sutra Book.

•

Contents

Section I: The Subtleties of Buddha Nature 1

Section II: Growth 37

Section III: Commentaries on Rinzai Zen Practice 81

Section IV: Teishos in the Rinzai Spirit 137

Appendix 193

Section I

The Subtleties of Buddha Nature

Introduction • 3
We Are Formed Temporarily • 5
The Something • 7
Differentiation • 9
Seeing the Really Real • 11
Where is Home? • 13
Flowers of the Universe • 15
Expressing the Entire Matter • 17
Who Is It? • 19
"Minutely Subtle" • 23
Virtually Dead • 25
Without Form • 29
Mu is Doing Bob • 31
Impermanence • 33

Introduction

Most people will agree that the material in this section is very difficult. It is, however, very important to a study of the Rinzai Zen tradition, and to understanding the root of Zen Buddhism.

Some would argue that it's unnecessary to present this material at all in written form. An understanding of Buddha Nature, they say, will unfold naturally in the course of Zen practice.

Others argue that, particularly for Westerners, the intellect and the imagination must be engaged to sustain an arduous and lengthy practice. Reading and study fill a need and serve as reference. For many of the people attracted to Zen Buddhism, words provide the first wondrous glimpse of a new vista.

Buddha Nature, This Matter, the concepts presented in the following pages, *are* difficult.

Don't worry about it. One way or another, sooner or later, you will understand.

•

We Are Formed Temporarily

Almost all of us have some kind of rank or position: committee chair, administrative assistant, deputy superintendent. We have some kind of title: husband, wife, student of Dharma, *sesshin* participant, *tenzo, jisha*. Or at least, we have a name. So, what we consider "self" has a name, a nationality, and titles. But Master Rinzai says there is a True Man Without Rank. Instead of using the words Buddha Nature, or True Nature, or some other religious term, Rinzai invented the phrase True Man Without Rank. Out of This! — or, True Man Without Rank! — we are temporarily formed in this way or that way, with temporary names and ranks. But because we are deceived — deluded — and think that the temporary being is real, or permanent, the True Man Without Rank is forgotten.

•

The Something

As human beings, we experience greed, anger, jealousy, folly, envy, confusion, desire, anxiety, frustration.... We want to be free of these very uncomfortable feelings and situations.

Some of us are fortunate enough to hear about Zen practice and when we begin, we think: I'm practicing Zen, or I'm doing *zazen*, or I'm doing Mu, which is another word for Buddha Nature. We think I, I am, I do.

But gradually, we begin to realize that there is a Something. That Something was there before we were born, before our present formation, and it will still be there after our transformation. It is a Something that is constantly active. At first we think that that Something is somewhere else, but the fact is, that Something of beginningless beginnings and endless ends, vast, boundless, mysterious, is centered here in ourselves.

Soen Roshi often said, "There are so many Zen centers nowadays. But the true Zen center is here in our *hara*." Each one of our hara-s, our solar plexus, our center of balance, is the center of Mu, of Buddha Nature.

And yet at the same time we say that Buddha Nature, our True Nature, is everything, everywhere — "...in any (or every) event, in any moment, and in any place...".

Among all the mysterious things in the world, Buddha Nature is the most mysterious — the most incomprehensible, ungrabbable, indefinable. So we do zazen, asking deeply, What is my True Nature? Where is it? Where is It?

Once we do come to an awareness of the vivid activity of the Something, we will be able not only to answer where? what? who? which? is It, but we will also be free from many anxieties, and especially from our spiritual anxieties.

•

Differentiation

This matter, or This Matter, or Buddha Nature, is very subtle.

I hope you understand that essentially speaking — speaking on the level of essence — there is no Buddha apart from us. There is no Dharma apart from us. (Or, no *activity* of Buddha Nature.) We are none other than the manifestation, revelation, temporary formation of This Matter, called Buddha, Buddha Nature, or in our training, Mu. And therefore, apart from us, there is no such thing as Buddha.

Language is so tricky. To say, this part of my glasses is a separately nameable part of my glasses — the lens — is true. But at the same time, it is an integral and inseparable part of what I speak of as "my glasses". The speck of dust *is* the three thousand galaxies of worlds. "When I sit, the universe sits." You *are* Buddha Nature.

However, however — as we can see, as we can hear, there are glasses, paper, microphone, bowing mat, flower, altar buddha, you, and uncountable things are here, and they are all different. Different forms, different names, different functions, different lives. Relatively, or existentially speaking, everything is differentiated.

Essentially speaking, we are Buddha. Relatively speaking, we are bumpkins. These opposites — enlightenment and delusion, buddhas and bumpkins — seem to be contradictions. But, like love and hate, they are one thing, yet two aspects. Love and hate are inseparable. So are Buddha and bumpkin. So are delusion and enlightenment, *samsara* and *nirvana,* birth and death. Sometimes it may seem to us that the real is not rational!

In any particular moment, when we say the word "Buddha," it has a positive feeling, while "bumpkin" has a negative feeling. Or more accurately, one is preferable. Or one is likeable and the other is not. The fact is, when each word is uttered, it has its own nuance and implication and connotation. The moment it is uttered, our mind, for some reason, goes and sticks to it. "Buddha" is great.

"Bumpkin" is no good. But bumpkins and buddhas are not two different things. The problem is the sticky nature of our mind.

If I say to you all, raise your hand if you are bumpkin, perhaps one hundred percent of you will raise your hands. If I ask, "Do you think you are Buddha?" some people will say, "Well — I doubt it." So we think we are more bumpkin than Buddha. Essentially, we are Buddha. But both are true. Love and hate toward the same person doesn't make sense, but it happens frequently. Essentially love, temporarily hate. This is what Buddhists say. Essentially compassion, temporarily, once in a great while, bitterness. But they are the same thing. This is not "dualism". This is just two aspects of One Matter, which we say is unnameable but which we call Mu.

•

Seeing the Really Real

A very difficult subject and a very deep philosophical statement is this: Buddhism sees this world as illusion.

We modern people, as materialistic individuals, think this world is real. It is so difficult for us to regard pain, for instance, as illusion. To regard it as illusion seems impossible. Pain is real! But what Rinzai and the patriarchs are saying throughout their teaching is, "Yes, we suffer. But the cause of suffering is misconception. And the misconception is that we regard illusion as real."

Perhaps the biggest point of our practice as human beings, as individuals born in the twentieth century, is to shift our understanding from the so-called "real" to the really real. As Master Rinzai is saying throughout the Rinzai Roku, if this shift is made, there will be emancipation.

"Followers of the Way, Mind is without form."

Mind is without form. These are not just words, but fact. But the fact has to be described in words, and we read it in printed letters and think that it's words. It's not words. It's a fact! "Mind is without form." You may resist this. You may fear losing control, or losing your being. But understanding this is true insight.

Followers of the Way, Mind is without form.

Today's *teisho* talk is finished.

All other words are just extra. All the enlightened verses —

"To regard the form of no-form as form..."

"All composite things are like a dream, a fantasy, a bubble, a shadow..."

— these are extra.

But here are more words because we need more help.

"In the eye it is called seeing." In the ear it is called hearing. In the nose, it is odor. In the mouth, there is conversation. In the hand, grasping and seizing. In the feet, running and carrying. In the brain, thinking. At the beginning of so-called this life, it is so-to-speak born. At the end of so-called this life, it so-to-speak dies.

You are probably saying, "These Zen teachers' statements are not very logical." Without logic, our "left brain" is not convinced. But these Zen patriarchs are not trained in logic, and their statements are not at all rational. They are speaking from the fundamental level to our "right brain", to the less cultivated, less trained side of our understanding. With our "right brain", or intuitively, or on the essential level we will become convinced and there will be no confusion. "Mind is without form, and since Mind is without form, therefore wherever you are, you are emancipated."

It is at this point where zazen practice becomes so important. "Let them sit," they must be saying. And if the fish is hungry, it bites. If it isn't, it doesn't. When we are hungry for the truth, we become curious. When we have Great Curiosity for the really real — we bite. And this biting is zazen. Chewing. Training the right brain.

•

Where Is Home?

Mind, with a capital M, is the "he" of Master Rinzai's sentence: "He is the primal source of all the buddhas." Rinzai also refers often to "the one who". For instance: "Virtuous monks" — or virtuous ladies and gentlemen — "you must recognize the one who manipulates these reflections...."

Again, the problem of language. When we see "the one who" we cannot help but think there must be someone. But try to interpret it this way: You must recognize that nothing, no-thing, no thing, is the primal source of all the buddhas." Please do not be deceived by such expressions as "one" or "he".

The technical term for this "he" is *shunyata*, no-thing, nothing, no thing. Shunyata is a good word — a Sanskrit word — for Buddha Nature, or This Matter, or Universal Reality, or Universal Consciousness. But don't think of shunyata as a concept. It's a fact.

Shunyata. That is still a name, but we have to use a name. Nothing, not a thing exists as an entity. This is so difficult even to imagine. But there is a fact which we call "shunyata", or it can be called True Self, or it can be called God that created heaven and earth, that created everything.

What I'm talking about is not a "metaphysical" subject. It is very factual. I use the example of ocean and wave. They are the same thing in one sense, and yet different, and yet the same. They are inseparable. Therefore, sometimes we are speaking of this fundamental or essential reality, this shunyata matter, and at the same time, we may be speaking of this phenomenological or existential matter. This is where there are two, yet one, yet two.

Mind is no other than "this great universe", or Buddha Nature, which this Zen tradition calls Mu. And that Mu you will recognize as the primal source of all the buddhas and *bodhisattvas*, gods, deities. If you do recognize this — and to some degree everybody will reach this kind of experience — then "every place is the home to which the Follower of the Way returns." Or, as is said in Master

Hakuin's Song of Zazen: "Whether going or returning, you cannot be any place else."

This is not someone else's story. It's *your* matter. Whether going or returning, whether staying or departing, you cannot be any place else than home. That is the original, eternal, while at the same time temporary, home to which all Followers of the Way return. So there's no need ever to feel estranged. Wherever you are, that is your home.

•

The Flowers of the Universe

I asked Soen Roshi which of his *haiku* he thought was the best. Without hesitation he replied, "All beings are flowers, blooming in a blooming universe."

Hana no yo no
Hana no yoh naru
Hito bakari

Flower — not snow, not moon, not maple, not golden wind — Spring flower. All beings, whether sentient or non-sentient, animate or inanimate, are as beautiful as a flower blooming each moment, in each place, with all its heart.

Some of you may have suffered separation, and that separation too is like a flower. Death too is like a flower, like a blooming flower. Confusion, pain, all kinds of things we might categorize as negative, are also as vital as a blooming flower. Only when this is testified to, then we greedy, lazy human beings may be able to become contented and happy. Otherwise, we may say, "I am doing Mu in order to have *my kensho, my* enlightenment experience." That is sad, really sad.

The flowering blooming flower. Each thing, each event — a meeting is an event, separation is an event, joy is an event, old age is a phenomenon, catching cold is a phenomenon, low bloodpressure is a phenomenon. Some we prefer, some we don't. We have preferences. But Sosan Ganchi Zenji said:

The perfect way knows no difficulties
Except that it refuses to show preferences; . . .
To set up what you like against what you dislike —
This is the disease of the mind.

With Mu-realization, when we are free from categorizing, even war, even the atom bomb, good and evil, right and wrong — all are blooming flowers.

•

Expressing the Entire Matter

Hogen said to Shisho, "What is the meaning of 'In the myriad forms, a single body is revealed'?"
(In Japanese this is, *"Banzo shichu doku ro shin."*)
Shisho raised his teaching whisk.
Hogen said, "What you just did is in imitation of our teacher, Chokei."

Imitation.
What is *your* understanding of the "single body revealed"? May I see it? Saying Mu, mu, mu is a very good thing, but not if you just imitate Joshu. What is *your* understanding? Has a dog Buddha Nature? What would *you* say?
Shisho had no answer.
Hogen said, "Do you sweep the myriad forms away?"
"No."
Well of course, no. But this is an inseparable matter. Of course you cannot sweep them away, but to say "no" does not express the entire matter, does not imply both sweeping and non-sweeping.
Hogen said, "Then your understanding of the myriad forms in a single body seems dualistic."
Shisho's Dharma brothers all said, "Sweep them away."
But transcending these answers, Hogen said, *"Banzo shichu doku ro shin NI!!*
What's the difference between Ni!, Mu!, and Ho! which we often chant when we walk (*kinhim*)? Ho, Ni, Mu — these are all expressions of something which is impossible to express, yet needs to be expressed. It is the same thing as "Dong!" on the gong. As "Whack!" on the lectern.
After all these things become clear, then you will know that even coughing, even moving, and even raindrops falling...sshhhssh...are the same as Mu and Ni.
"In the myriad forms, a single body is revealed."

•

Who Is It?

The *koan* is an expression of Buddha Nature at a particular time and place, in particular circumstances. Although different individuals appear in the "stories", and the actions and expressions of the individuals are different, it is Buddha Nature that we are talking about.

One koan (Mumonkan, Case 45) is called, Hoen's Who Is He?

Goso Hoen Zenji's name appears in our lineage chant. His disciple was Engo Kokugon Zenji, who compiled the Blue Cliff Collection (Hekigan Roku) of koans. These teacher-student relationships may not mean anything to some of you, but these Dharma relationships are mysterious and precious.

> One day, Goso Hoen said, "Even Shakyamuni Buddha and Maitreya Bodhisattva are servants of that one. Tell me, who is that one?"

Shakyamuni Buddha is the founder of so-called Buddhism. Maitreya Bodhisattva, the future bodhisattva, is like the Messiah in the Jewish tradition, I think. Both Shakyamuni and Maitreya and all the patriarchs are all servants of *that* one. Who is *that* one? Or, who is this? Who is he? Who is that one? Who is it? What is It?

We call it Mu. Many of us are working with this Mu. In Mumon's verse for Case 44 in the koan collection called The Gateless Gate, he says, "It helps you wade across the river when the bridge is down. It accompanies you to the village on a moonless night." A very beautiful verse.

It. By now you all know what "it" means — Buddha Nature. This is very slippery. Very elusive. Very difficult to pinpoint. Buddha Nature, Mu, helps you cross the river when the bridge is broken. The human journey is a pilgrimage. We are all pilgrims, and on the way there are hills, mountains, fields, deserts, and rivers. To be more precise, anxieties, frustrations, confusion, death, separation, illness, insecurity, broken bridges whether we like it or not. It helps us — Mu helps us, Mu-realization helps us — to cross the river when the bridge is broken. Quite often the bridge is broken.

Once in a great while we can cross a river without a broken bridge. The percentage is three-tenths of one percent. The traditional Japanese saying is that of the one thousand things you may do, you'll be truly contented with only three. That's average. But we greedy beings think that eighty percent should go our way. Therefore we become frustrated and angry. If you have to cross a thousand bridges on your spiritual pilgrimage, only three will be passable without impediment. If we look at it this way, we are grateful and have nothing to complain about. If things go bad, we can say, "Oh, it's one of those 997."

It helps you cross the river when the bridge is down. Mu helps you. Realization, or understanding of Buddha Nature, helps you. Mystery — it's the only word I can think of. It is a mystery. Mysterious Mu helps you. "It accompanies you when you return to the village on a moonless night." On a dark night, Mu accompanies you, always — in particular, to return to your own original village. It gives you direction, like a flashlight.

When Goso Hoen Zenji said, "Tell me, who is that one?" one of the monks stood up and answered, "John, Bob, Mary, Nancy." Goso said, "Fine."

Engo Kokugon Zenji, who was Goso Hoen's Dharma heir, said later, "I think you should be more careful confirming an answer." Goso said, "All right."

The following day, the same monk came to *dokusan* and Goso asked the same question. The monk said, "Well I told you yesterday. I said, Bob and John and Nancy and Mary."

Goso said, "No, no."

"But you said yes, yesterday."

Goso said, "Yesterday I said yes, but today I'm saying no."

When the monk heard Goso say, "Today I say no," he truly understood That One.

If you can really see That One with perfect clarity, it is like meeting your own father on Fifth Avenue. You don't need to ask whether you recognize him or not. Needless to say, we are talking about our Buddha Nature.

However strenuous this practice of zazen may be, no matter how difficult — I cannot imagine this life, this pilgrimage, without it.

•

"Minutely Subtle"

Here is a story about Yamamoto Gempo Roshi.

There is a Rinzai priest, the Reverend Matsubara, and the nearest English word for him is preacher. He speaks very well. He often went with Gempo Roshi and gave a talk at a gathering that was not a sesshin.

This time, it happened that Gempo Roshi could not be present during the talk. The weather was terrible and even though the talk had been announced long in advance, not as many people gathered as the temple had expected. In fact, only three showed up. But the Reverend Matsubara spoke as though there were two hundred or three hundred people in the audience.

Gempo Roshi saw him later and said, "My attendant monk told me that because of this terrible storm, only three people came to hear you. Nevertheless, you spoke as though it was a full audience. Let me ask you," said Gempo Roshi, "suppose only one showed up. Would you still speak in the same manner?"

"Yes, I would."

"Suppose nobody showed up, then what?"

The Rev. Matsubara said, "Then I would not speak."

Immediately, Gempo Roshi said, "That's no good! Do you do zazen because of your friends? Can't you sit alone?"

"Yes, I can."

"Do you do the *Nembutsu* because someone else is there to chant Namu Amida Butsu? Can't you do it by yourself?"

"Of course I can."

"So," said Gempo Roshi. "Even if no one shows up, the pillars hear. The floors listen."

The same point can be made about the koto, the Japanese harp. It is made of kiri wood. This is a very soft wood, and only this wood can be used for the koto. Naturally, the koto-maker will search for the best kiri wood, and that is found in the deep mountains near a temple where it can hear the evening gong.

Our mind is so materialistically oriented that it is rather difficult for us to believe all these "minutely subtle" penetrations. For instance, your lack of care about the chanting of Morning Service, turning pages loudly, delaying the service — one second's delay of one person is the delay of perhaps forty people — this is your disruptive preaching.

This sensitivity, this "minutely subtle" training, must be understood or it doesn't matter how many years you sit, it will be for nothing.

It's not such a difficult thing. Rinzai spirit! You have to use your eyes, ears, nose, tongue and, most importantly, your brain.

Concern. Concern.

•

Vitally Dead

The "minutely subtle" activity of Buddha Nature is right in front of us, but for most people in the world the door is shut and they miss seeing it. They miss experiencing it.

In a way, we can say that zazen practice is the practice of opening that closed door so that each one of us can participate in the minutely subtle, and what I call "delicious", taste of Buddha Nature.

Sometimes we speak about ancient patriarchs, such as Shuzan Shonen Zenji, and sometimes we speak of modern patriarchs such as Gempo Roshi, Yasutani Roshi, Nyogen Senzaki, and Soen Roshi. And sometimes we speak of living human beings, such as ourselves. But again, we're talking about nothing but subtle Buddha Nature.

> Shuzan Shonen Zenji was *shikaryo*, head monk, a very responsible position at Fuketsu Ensho Zenji's monastery. One day, he was working together with Fuketsu Zenji when suddenly the teacher began to cry. The shikaryo said, "Why are you crying?"
>
> Fuketsu said, "Ever since Shakyamuni Buddha's time, the Buddhadharma has been transmitted. But nowadays only an extremely limited number of people truly appreciate the beauty of Buddha Nature. Since Rinzai Gigen Zenji's time, four generations have already passed and Rinzai's dynamism is now getting weaker and weaker. I am very concerned about the future of Buddhadharma."
>
> The head monk saw the tears and was moved to say, "May I do something?"
>
> "Yes. I'm counting on you, but you are not doing enough zazen practice."
>
> Shuzan said, "From today, I will give my life to the Dharma."

I love this. What does he mean, "...give my life to the Dharma"?

Many of us are searching for something really worthy to commit ourselves to, and we windowshop for this and that and somehow we cannot find a This-Is-It! We hesitate about committing ourselves. "Is my profession truly worthy? Is *kensho*, enlightenment, guaranteed? I'm unsure; I have reservations."

Actually, it works the other way around. Unless we commit ourselves, nothing will happen!

Some of you say, "How does one know whether this or that is worthy of commitment or not?"

This is where bumpkin logic and Buddha Nature logic differ. Somehow, if we give ourselves to the Dharma, Dharma will give itself to us. This is how Buddha Nature functions. Unless you give yourself, no matter how many hundreds of thousands of sesshins you attend, a real breakthrough may not take place. Your chanting may become wonderful; you may strike the gong beautifully; your sitting posture may be as beautiful as a statue of the Buddha. But as far as the realization of Buddha Nature is concerned, without unconditional commitment, without dedication, without one hundred percent Mu, nothing will happen. Even in your first sesshin, your first sitting period, with one hundred percent conviction, faith, dedication, MUUUuuuu.....!

So Shuzan said to his teacher, "I will give myself to the Dharma."

Here is an illustration of what "I will give myself to the Dharma" means.

Sometimes I hang a scroll at the left of the altar with a poem by Soen Roshi. The "ordinary" translation is,

Crawling out of the Dead Sea,
My body,
Glittering Spring water.

If you interpret this haiku in the ordinary sense, you may think that Soen Roshi went to Jerusalem and one day he went to the Dead Sea. He stripped off his clothes and swam. It was Springtime. He came out of the Dead Sea and, in the Spring sunshine, before he took a shower, his body was glittering with Spring water. Period.

And this was true. But the greatest enjoyment of a haiku is to interpret it in a spiritual dimension.

The Dead Sea is not only in Israel; it's your cushion. But you're not yet even floating — you're afraid to enter the Dead Sea. You prefer to enter a Paradise Sea. Dead Sea! Dead! Once you enter the Dead Sea, there's no fear, no resistance, no expectation, no calculation, no judgment, no right, no wrong — that's what "Dead Sea" means. And then, once dead, then crawling — this is wonderful! — *crawling* out. And there, Spring sunshine, glittering water, glittering light — "*Attha dipa, viharatha, attha sarana* . . . You are the light itself...!"

This is one of Soen Roshi's masterpieces. Crawling out from death, the dead condition, the zazen-dead condition, my body and mind, glittering Spring light and water. The implication is, unless you jump into the Dead Sea, dead zazen — not dead and lifeless, but *vitally* dead, not deceased dead — it doesn't matter whether you open your eyes or close your eyes, put your hands in this *mudra* or that mudra. It doesn't matter! What does matter, however, is this center, this hara. Enter *this* dead, where there is no judgment, no expectation, no body, no mind, no feeling, even no Mu, nothing, nothing, not, not, not!

Then, crawling out, you'll find something different — very different — where this delicious taste of Buddha Nature can be appreciated and life can be so interesting.

So, "Crawling out from the Dead Sea, my body, glittering Spring water."

Right now instead of crawling out, what we have to do is crawl into the Dead Sea, to go into that vitally dead, utter darkness, first.

Master Hakuin said, "Young monks, if you truly die on the cushion and realize birthlessness and deathlessness, you will never die again."

•

Without Form

"This physical body of yours, composed of the four great elements, can neither expound the Dharma nor listen to it; your spleen and stomach, liver and gallbladder, can neither expound the Dharma nor listen to it...."

It's a big subject, that of body and spirit. Everybody knows the German mystic, Meister Eckhart. When we read him, we know immediately that he is speaking the truth. What he said was not from his accumulation of knowledge but came out of what people call his mystical experience. I am positively sure he was a profoundly enlightened individual.

But even Meister Eckhart says nothing about the body. Nothing about how to sit, about posture, about how to breathe, how to concentrate.

This is where Zen Buddhism is quite different from Eckhart, although the Rinzai Roku (the sayings and doings of Master Rinzai) doesn't say how to do zazen either. But mention of the body appears from time to time, as in the beginning quotation, and we consider body and spirit as inseparable and equally indispensable. At the beginning of our practice we say, sitting posture, quiet walking, regulated breath — and now we are adding yoga exercise — lead us to what could be called mystical experience, although I personally don't like that expression. To true understanding, or to genuine insight, would be better expressions.

But even though the body is important, the spleen, stomach, liver, gallbladder, heart, kidney, brain, muscle, bone, and so on, can neither expound the Dharma nor listen to it. You may say, "Well I expound the Dharma with my tongue and I listen to the Dharma through my ears." This is the bumpkin vista, not the fundamental vista.

Master Rinzai goes on.

> "...the empty sky can neither expound the Dharma nor listen to it. Then just what can expound the Dharma and listen to it? This very you, standing before me without any form, just shining — this can expound the Dharma and listen to it!"

According to our bumpkin vista, we have a form. For many, many years we have been convinced that this particular form is "me", "myself". We are attached to it, and are even afraid to lose it. But real self, real Self, is not, and does not have, this form. It's formless! This is where the problem comes in.

"This very you, standing before me without any form, simply shining!" No form. And therefore, it can be *any* form, according to karmic combination. According to karmic combination temporarily, at this moment, I have this form. This form is constantly being transformed. X years from now, I will be transformed into ashes, another form.

No matter how beautiful you may appear, if you consider your body as form, no matter how much you try to shine, it's not real shining. "Understand it this way, and you are not different from a patriarch-buddha." You are no different from any kind of bodhisattva. *Not* understanding it this way, even if you have a PhD degree, you are very, very different from a patriarch-buddha. Not only that — true serenity, true peace of mind, real imperturbability, cannot be obtained.

We may say that we want this or that — endless greed goes on — but finally, this is what we really want. "This very you, standing before me without any form, just shining, can expound the Dharma and listen to it. Understand it this way and you are no different from a patriarch-buddha." This understanding is what we all want, after all.

If you see it this way, this is insight.

•

Mu Is Doing Bob

One of the important teachings of Buddhism is known as *in ga mu nin.* "Mu nin" means, no person. There is no person but only "in ga", only karma. We normally think and see the other side of this truth, that there is a person. He or she as a person exists, and this person has his or her own karma, and that is not completely wrong. But it is only half true. The other half is the half we miss.

You've heard the Diamond Sutra many times, but let me read one paragraph, and with great concentration, listen to this part.

> Subhuti, bodhisattvas should discipline their thoughts as follows. All living beings, whether born from eggs, from wombs, from moisture, or by transformation, whether with form or without form, whether in a state of thinking or exempt from thought-necessity, or wholly beyond all thought-realms — all these are caused by me to attain unbounded liberation-nirvana. Why is this, Subhuti? It is because no bodhisattva who is a real bodhisattva cherishes the idea of an ego-entity, a personality, a being or a separated individuality. And why is this, Subhuti? Because if a bodhisattva holds the idea of an ego-entity, a personality, a being or a separated individuality, then he is not a true bodhisattva, an enlightened being.

Normally we hold to the idea of a being. There was Nakagawa Soen Roshi, having an ego-entity, a special, eccentric personality, a separated Japanese individuality. And now that individuality has gone, thus we think. But that's an upside-down, bumpkin view. We do zazen to help erase this upside-down view. In truth, there is no distinction, no separation, between so-called Mr. A and so-called Mr. B, or between the so-called state of living and the so-called state of having died. When this is realized, then we see the missing half of the truth and there is a total picture.

So it's incorrect for you to say, "My name is Bob and I am doing Mu-practice." You should say, "Mu is doing Mu" or "Mu is doing Bob."

•

Impermanence

It says in the Diamond Sutra that if we understand at least one particular verse — comprehend it, explain it, and expound it — that deed is far more meritorious than a donation of all the treasures in the seven worlds.

> Now, in what manner may he explain it to others?
> By detachment from appearances, abiding in real Truth.
>> All composite things are like a dream,
>> A phantasm, a bubble, and a shadow,
>> Are like a dewdrop and a flash of lightning.
>> They are thus to be regarded.

Another translation is:

> So you should think of all this fleeting world:
> A star at dawn, a bubble in a stream,
> A flash of lightning in a summer cloud,
> A flickering lamp, a phantom, and a dream.

Even to chant this short verse again and again during zazen would be one of the ways to penetrate This Matter.

Let us think a little more deeply about this Impermanence that is expressed so poetically in the Diamond Sutra. To do this, first we must say something about causation.

The essence of the Wisdom Sutra is condensed into the following lines.

"All phenomena are born because of causation. Since they are born through causation, each phenomenon has no entity. Because each phenomenon has no entity, there is in fact no coming and no going, no loss and no gain, and therefore this is named shunyata."

Especially when we sit, we see that all kinds of phenomena, external and internal, appear and disappear. For instance, I'm catching a cold. This is one phenomenon. Why am I catching a cold? Maybe this or that reason can be found. But still, why? why? The point is, this phenomenon is produced by causation. One cause was produced by another cause, and the first cause is unknown.

The present phenomenon, catching a cold, is a phenomenon, not an entity. "Like a dream, like a phantasm, like a bubble, like a shadow." Nor is any so-called "good" phenomenon an entity in itself. Nor is insight. Insight is not a fixed entity, but just (snap!) it so happens. In this place, at this time! True now, not yesterday, and most probably not tomorrow. Only in this place, at this time. Right here, right now. All phenomena, whether physical pain, or exceptionally lucid zazen, or emotional feelings, are phenomena, not entities. They are all impermanent.

Another way to say this is: each phenomenon is unprecedented, and unrepeatable. Similar things happen, but not the same things. Because of the similarity, we are deceived, and think they are the same.

All phenomena are like a dream, a phantasm. They exist, and yet are ungrabbable. Like a mist: there, but ungraspable. Dewdrop, flash of lightning. "So you should think of all this fleeting world." Fleeting world. Modern people don't use this term. But modern people have certainly witnessed the changes in Eastern Europe in recent years, for instance. When we can think, "This world is fleeting, this phenomenon is fleeting, not permanent," our viewpoint changes. A bubble in a stream — yes, we can see it as a phenomenon, and a few minutes later it's gone.

In Hakuin Zenji's Rohatsu Exhortations, Fifth Day, we read the story of Heishiro. He carved a stone buddha and placed it in the deep mountains near a waterfall. He sat down by the waterfall and watched the bubbles in the pool float a few feet and disappear, and some floated longer than a few feet and disappeared. And somehow watching these phenomena, these simplest phenomena, he was able to understand. All of a sudden he realized that this world is so fleeting and impermanent.

At home, he started doing zazen without being instructed. He shut the door of his room and sat down, grasping his hands, and opening his eyes widely. The feeling of this impermanence was so strong, and his zazen was naturally so strong, that within three days or so — forgetting to sleep, forgetting to eat — within only three days or so he was able to realize This Matter.

This is a very inspiring story.

Everybody knows, whether the Diamond Sutra says so or not, that this world is fleeting. A star at dawn, a bubble in a stream, are impermanent. A flash of lightning in a summer cloud is not an entity. A flickering lamp, a phantasm, and a dream. This is where we live.

I was thinking that while sitting in the zendo, though we cannot see bubbles in front of us, we do experience the changes of dawn, of twilight, of the wind, of the gong reverberating. If even for a short period of time, we can truly see these changing, fleeting phenomena, then "impermanence" is no longer merely a word. It becomes vivid.

In fact, impermanence *is* Buddha Nature.

•

Section II

Growth

Introduction • 39
Virtue • 41
The Readiness of Time • 43
Plain and Direct • 45
Compassion • 47
Drinking the Medicine • 49
That Great Cloud • 51
Gratitude • 53
Five Joys in the Dharma • 55
Eliminate the Negative • 57
Precepts • 59
A Slow Process • 63
You, and the Four Elements • 67
Appreciating the Fourfold Wisdom • 71

Introduction

Students can be trained but should not be bound.

My hope is that each student can grow freely, changing freely according to each one's manifestation, without restriction by the teacher and without dependence on the teacher.

This takes patience by both teacher and student because it is a process without end.

Beginningless, and endless.

•

Virtue

When Rinzai, who eventually became a famous Chinese Zen master, had gained clear insight under the guidance of Obaku Kiun Zenji, he traveled widely to visit various Zen teachers.

At Ryoko's monastery he said, "Without unsheathing the point of a weapon, how can one win the battle?" Or: without saying a word, how can you be convincing?

Here is a story on this subject. In Kyoto, there is a monastery called Myoshin-ji. It's a huge place with forty-nine subtemples. Every few years there is a different abbot. Once a month, or maybe twice, the abbot gives a Dharma talk for the priests of all the temples. At one time there was a new fashion: monks and priests shaved their heads but grew their moustaches. So each new abbot said, "Shave your moustache." But for some reason nobody paid attention. One day, a new abbot was installed — Kogen Ishitsu Toyoda I Dokutan Roshi. According to tradition, he gave his teisho and all the monks and priests — with their shaven heads but with moustaches — were gathered in the hall. And instead of saying, "Oh you *must* shave your moustaches," he said in a soft voice, "Nowadays every priest in Myoshin-ji has a moustache."

By the following day, everybody had shaved.

So now we have to think. It's not what's said, or how it's said. It's who said it. There's no reason to be upset if someone doesn't listen to you or obey you. A Japanese would say to himself, "It's the deficiency of my virtue, that's why he doesn't listen." In Dokutan Roshi's case it was his *toku,* his virtue, that made these people shave. Without consulting each other! The point is this: don't be upset. When the time comes and when you are ready, somehow things will go in the way you wish.

So, without unsheathing the point of the weapon, how can one win a battle? Without arguing, how can one win the dispute? Dokutan Roshi's story is a good example. Master Rinzai asked, "Without saying a word, how can you persuade others?" This is especially difficult for us to understand nowadays, especially in America. Even though there is that proverb — "Speech is silver but silence is golden" — in reality, speech is indispensable and silence is regarded as something stupid.

This is a wonderful koan for each one of us to think about deeply. "Without saying a word" or with few, *few* words, how can you "win"? How can you convince others?

•

The Readiness of Time

There is a key concept for which I use the phrase "the readiness of time."

When something will happen, we don't know, but it will be in the readiness of time.

And, moment after moment, This! This! is the readiness of time.

Perhaps we cannot pin down what the starting date in the development of some project was, but it developed in the readiness of time.

We are all time-oriented people, speaking relatively. We want to know when something started and when it will end. To this kind of question, Dogen Kigen Zenji gave a wonderful answer. He said not to ask such a question because we have no way of answering. All we can say is, from the beginningless beginning to the endless end.

But unless we deepen our zazen, we're not satisfied with this kind of ambiguous answer. We want to know *exactly*. Perhaps after several years of zazen, you may be able to accept this very truthful expression: from the beginningless beginning to the endless end. When Buddha Nature is ready, or in the readiness of time.

Generally speaking, we are not strong. We are rather greedy and rather lazy. We are fearful, and we have confusions and anxieties. But when we can testify to, and sense, see, and feel Buddha Nature itself, these inner anxieties will be allayed. The reason why our anxiety is so acute is that we don't know what we really are. Once that is settled by realizing true Buddha Nature, we can calm down. There may still be greed, jealousy, anger, and other problems resulting both from our past habits and from *karma,* but one essential problem is solved. This is why Shakyamuni Buddha and all the patriarchs in the Zen tradition repeatedly emphasize the importance of realizing your True Nature.

When I speak this way, you hope this realization will happen this afternoon, or at the latest this evening, or at least by the end of sesshin. If that happens that's fine, but you must also remember what I said earlier. If you really want to know the true meaning of Buddha Nature, you must understand the readiness of time. If you do understand this, all kinds of anxieties will diminish.

•

Plain and Direct

It is said that Rinzai, one monk among seven hundred at Obaku's monastery, was "plain and direct in his behavior." This means behaving without selfconsciousness, without hesitation, without calculation. Very naturally. And without thinking about a reward.

We have such fear and distrust — this is a modern disease. If it is guaranteed that some action will be worth our while, worth our energy and concern, then we do it. But in Zen we say, become a fool. A fool doesn't calculate, isn't "clever". He has no desires, anxieties, and frustrations. He is, as told in this description of Rinzai, plain and direct in his behavior.

•

Compassion

Visiting Vimalakirti was not an easy job for Manjushri, as we read in the Vimalakirti Sutra. Vimalakirti was quite tough, profound, lucid, and knowledgeable. Twelve others had refused to visit him.

This is not just Manjushri's problem. If we refuse to do something difficult or a job we don't like, we will not make progress. It's easy for us to visit someone who is comfortable to be with or who is not complicated. But that doesn't help us to grow. So Manjushri accepted the Buddha's order and went to visit Vimalakirti.

While he and Vimalakirti were talking, Manjushri asked, "Why are you sick?"

Vimalakirti answered — and this is a famous line — "Because all beings are sick, therefore I am sick."

What does this mean? Many of you may think, I am healthy. I'm not catching a cold; my stomach is fine; nothing is bothering me; I'm not sick at all. But according to the Buddhist way of looking at things, there are two kinds of sickness. One is physical and mental. The other is "...greed, anger, and delusion". Greed is sickness; anger is sickness; delusion is sickness. Misconception, of what self really is, is sickness. Therefore, we are all sick. Hence, Vimalakirti said that because all beings are sick, I am sick.

Soen Roshi says this in a haiku that can be translated as: "The pain of the planet is my pain."

Vimalakirti knew that Manjushri needed to understand this sickness. And then, to understand compassion.

•

Drinking the Medicine

Of course Shakyamuni Buddha is a very important person, and so is Bodhidharma, and Eno Dai Kan Zenji, the Sixth Patriarch, and in fact there is no patriarch who is not important. But Rinzai Gigen Zenji was the founder of the Rinzai School and that is especially important to us.

It is a strenuous practice we do compared to other schools but our strenuous effort builds a strong foundation.

The Golden Age of Chinese Zen was the Tang Dynasty and then the Sung Dynasty. Rinzai — Lin Chi is his name in Chinese — was born between these. As we find with most of the patriarchs, when Rinzai was young he was bright and sincere. Evidently there are two things in common for all the teachers of outstanding genius of the past: brilliance and sincerity.

At first Rinzai studied general Buddhist philosophy, which is of course important, but at some point he became frustrated. It made sense, but so what? It sounded good, but so what? It must be correct — it sounded correct — but what about his anxieties?

No matter how many books I may read, no matter how clearly I may understand Buddhist philosophy, and no matter that I have accumulated endless intellectual materials in my brain and have all the notions and pictures in my mind of the Buddha's sayings and the bodhisattvas' sayings — what about everyday life? What about everyday feelings, everyday regrets, anger, resentment, greed, and many, many, many other problems of my own daily life? Buddhists say there is delusion. They say that the existence of the self is a delusion. But when I sit, there is pain and the pain is very concrete. When I slap at my body, I feel it is tangible. This is not a metaphysical existence.

Almost everyone will confront this confusion between what we read in Buddhism and what we concretely seem to be. These two things somehow don't connect.

For Rinzai, there was confusion and frustration because there was no *gyo*, no practice, no daily work of connection between philosophy and experience. Whether it is painful or otherwise stressful, what we are doing is gyo. Even though we don't exactly understand it, there is less frustration if we do it. In my opinion, to state it briefly in one word, Buddhism *is* gyo — practice.

So Rinzai "changed his robe" from another school of Buddhism to Zen and traveled to the monastery of Obaku (Huang Po) Kiun Zenji. Rinzai had said to himself, "Intellectual understanding is like the prescription for medicine; it's not the medicine itself. What I'm going to do now is drink the medicine."

What you're doing now, what we're doing now — with great agony inside, with confusion, resistance, pain, fear, self-pity — is drinking the medicine. Doing, doing, doing. Without doing, nothing happens.

You may say, "But I have been doing this for x years and still nothing happens." X years on and off, most of the time, off. But even Shakyamuni Buddha, religious genius that he was, with great motivation, and even extreme "doing" — although he realized very quickly that asceticism is too extreme, so he chose the Middle Way of doing — still did six years "on" of zazen after that. And he opened the Way for all of us.

So don't be impatient, don't be impatient. It's quite understandable, but don't be impatient. You may think: "I cannot see much progress. What am I doing? Am I not wasting my time?"

But this is too narrow a viewpoint in the long, long life of the universe. Nothing is wasted. You are not wasting your time.

•

That Great Cloud

Feelings arise — love and hate, jealousy, envy, fear, feeling, feeling, feeling. Of course we are animals of feeling. Likes, dislikes. But because of feelings, "wisdom is barred" says Master Rinzai.

Today is a beautiful day, sunshine, blue sky. It is a peaceful day. But when emotion comes, there comes a great cloud and the world becomes dark. Even the sunshine cannot penetrate that great cloud. Then wisdom is hidden.

I don't think Rinzai is saying, "You must not feel, you must not think." What he is asking is that we not become slaves of emotion, that we not become slaves of thinking.

This is where zazen comes in; this is where Mu comes in. This is where backbone and discipline come in. Zazen is training. Feelings appear, disappear, return, leave This is natural. But remember that feelings are impermanent and train not to become the *slave* of feeling.

Otherwise, "...men transmigrate through the three realms and undergo all kinds of suffering." We have had enough of that suffering and we would like to be free from it. Master Rinzai is saying that when we are not slaves of feeling, we don't have to undergo all kinds of suffering.

•

Gratitude

Experiencing and expressing gratitude is an important part of our teaching. Japanese Buddhists call it *ho on,* or "requiting beneficence". Let me explain a little of what this is.

We cannot live alone. We need people's support, we need food to eat, we need air to breathe, we need water to drink, fire to heat, we need friendship...so many, many things. And yet we don't often express our gratitude when these needs are satisfied. For instance, it's not the particular ways in which parents support you that is important, but it is the fact of their support that is important. That fact should be recognized and felt by children as gratitude. A student should feel some sense of gratitude towards the teacher.

Sometimes children cannot express this gratitude to their parents, but can give care and concern to their children. Thus it is transmitted from one generation to another.

To wind, and water, and food and other things, we should have a grateful attitude. "First, let us reflect on our own work, and the effort of those who brought us this food." This is the first line of the mealtime grace.

Ananda said, "With my whole heart I shall serve all beings throughout the myriad worlds."

This is "ho on", the expression of gratitude.

•

Five Joys in the Dharma

In the Vimalakirti Sutra, the twelfth student of Shakyamuni Buddha to be asked to visit Vimalakirti was Jisei Bodhisattva. He and Vimalakirti talked about the five joys in the Dharma.

Through our eyes, we prefer to see something beautiful rather than something ugly. Beautiful scene, beautiful painting. Through our ears, beautiful sound, music. Through our nose, great fragrance, like incense. And so on. The body desires something beautiful, comfortable, pleasurable.

But Vimalakirti told Jisei Bodhisattva that there are Five Dharma Joys or Pleasures.

The first is to believe in the Buddha, or in modern terms, to trust in our Buddha Nature.

The second is to hear the Dharma teaching.

The third is to make offerings to friends and *sangha* or community. The joy of giving. This is *so* important.

The fourth is to respect the teacher.

And the fifth Joy sounds very odd — the joy of changing one's face.

The first day of sesshin, look in the mirror. The last day, look again. Yes, your beard is longer, your hair is unwashed, but you can also see that your face has changed. With real zazen, you can't help but show a change.

You know, Abraham Lincoln is supposed to have said that up to the age of thirty-nine, one is not responsible for one's face. But on the morning of the fortieth birthday, one is totally responsible for one's face. You never heard this story? It is well known abroad.

Confucius said, at the age of forty we should no longer be deluded. Perhaps Confucius and Abraham Lincoln and Vimalakirti were all saying the same thing.

Experience the Five Joys in the Dharma before you are a day older.

•

Eliminate the Negative

Master Rinzai says, "As I see it, there are none who are not emancipated."

The problem is that many of you think, "Oh, Master Rinzai is great, but I am not yet emancipated. I assume that some day in the future I will be, but as of now I am not."

Many of us think: I'm terrible; I'm not there yet; I'm full of delusion. I'm not yet emancipated, I'm not enlightened.

But it will not help you to cling to "I'm bad, I'm terrible" and at the very same time expect to be relieved of your suffering.

Go out! Breathe some fresh air, look up at the cloudless sky, inhale deeply and exhale completely. Free yourself from this good-and-bad thinking. Come back to your zazen in a neutral condition, and fearlessly and unconditionally do Mu. If you can drop off your negative thinking so as to leave yourself in a more neutral condition, and if you can do what Dharma asks you to do without judgmental thoughts, then kensho, insight, and emancipation will not be long in visiting you.

•

Precepts

There are three Sanskrit words that you should know: *sutra; shastra; vinaya.*

"Vinaya" is usually translated as precepts.

"Sutra" means, a written record of the Buddha's teachings. Sutras are not necessarily his exact words but were written by enlightened students, and were based on the spirit of the Buddha's teaching. The Lotus Sutra is a good example, or the Heart Sutra.

The "shastras" are commentaries.

These writings comprise The Tripitaka — the triple writings.

Rinzai, when he discovered that all these works were "merely displays of doctrine in written words," threw them away and practiced zazen.

For us, it is too early to throw them away. Before we throw them away, at least we should understand the basic matter of the vinaya.

In Japanese, the word is *kai*. In English, precepts. In Sanskrit, vinaya. I have spoken about the ten precepts many times. Perhaps therefore you have the impression that the ten precepts are the most fundamental statements of Buddhist thought. But the root of the ten precepts is *san ju jo kai*. San means three; ju means condensed; jo kai means purified precepts. It sounds complicated but it's very simple. The three condensed precepts are these.

> We vow to refrain from all action that creates attachments.
> We vow to make every effort to live our lives awake in truth.
> We vow to live to benefit all beings.

There is a famous story about this. In China, there was a very well-known poet named Hakurakuten, and in those days there was a rather unusual Buddhist priest, Dorin. Dorin lived in a tree so people called him Nest Master. Hakurakuten wanted to know the essence of Buddhadharma, so one day he went to the tree and with a bow asked, "Sir, please teach me the essence of Buddhadharma."

Master Dorin said, "Refrain from all bad action. Engage in good action. And always purify your heart."

The poet was going to laugh. "Is that the quintessence of Buddhism?"

"Yes."

"Even an eight-year-old knows that."

"Yes. But even an eighty-year-old cannot do it."

And then Hakurakuten understood something of This Matter and he made a deep bow.

We may now think that these three are the root of the ten precepts, but there is one more root — the root of the root. In English, briefly, it is "to take refuge". We take refuge in the Buddha, in the Dharma, and in the Sangha. These are called the Three Refuges or the Three Treasures. *Buddham saranam gacchami, Dharmam saranam gacchami, Sangham saranam gacchami*. Whatever kind of Buddhist we are — Zen, Shingon, Tibetan, Theravadin — these are the essential kai, the essential precepts. They don't sound like precepts, but that's because we think that precepts say what to do or what not to do.

There are three different ways to interpret the Three Treasures.

One way is called, in Japanese, *itai san bo*. The Buddha, Dharma, and Sangha are not separate from each other. When we practice Mu, this Mu is Buddha. This Mu is Dharma. This Mu is Sangha. This is the most important interpretation and understanding. The three are one. The second way of interpretation is called *gen jen san bo*. This refers to the historical Three Treasures, we might say. Buddha is Shakyamuni Buddha who realized this Mu Universal Reality, and who preached the Dharma for forty-nine years. The Dharma is the teaching. And the Sangha was composed of his immediate students in India some 2500 years ago.

The third way of interpretation of the Three Treasures is, the transmission from generation to generation. The Buddha has passed away, so we use the statue or the scroll as a representation. The Dharma is the bird singing, the wind blowing, the chanting of the Kanzeon sutra, listening to teisho, gathering for Dharma discussion — Dharma activity. And the Sangha is composed of students of this generation.

To ensure the transmission from generation to generation we chant, "Let True Dharma Continue", Let True Dharma Continue. Or, *Namu Dai Bosa,* Namu Dai Bosa, or MU! All of these are the *nen* — the intense thought — that the Dharma will continue. One by one we may disappear, but let true Dharma continue!

Therefore, these Three Treasures are the most fundamental precept.

If there is any misunderstanding about Buddhism, it is our responsibility, our sangha responsibility, to clarify understanding. Then Buddhadharma will continue, and will be the oasis in the desert where thirsty travellers may drink and find rest.

Let's return to the ten precepts for a moment. I'm going to explain one point so that they will become somewhat clearer to you. Without clarity, it's too early to "throw them away...."

These ten precepts also can be looked at in three different ways: the Theravada or Hinayana way; the Mahayana way; and from the Buddha Nature or shunyata viewpoint.

Here is an example.

In the Theravada way, precepts are taken quite literally. Do not kill means, do not kill even insects or animals that may harm human life.

The Mahayana Buddhist applies deep compassion to this precept. As a result, there is often ambiguity in interpretation and action. If you are in Africa and a lion or tiger wants to bite you and your friends and your children, then you use your gun. The Theravada Buddhist says this is breaking the precept. The Mahayana Buddhist says it is not.

"Do not kill" from the Buddha Nature point of view is rather difficult to explain, but I would say this. As long as we have the dualistic notion that there is something to kill, a killer, and being-killed, then killing will be considered as breaking the precept. But if we have very profound insight into the nature of True Self in which there is no dualistic notion, we will see this precept from a very different viewpoint; we will see a different vista.

So do not throw away the written word before studying and thinking deeply. When you have done this, and after sufficient zazen training and experience, when the Dharma eye is clear, it will be possible to avoid being "fooled" by the various interpretations of the precepts while still respecting them.

•

A Slow Process

I have been talking to various Dharma brothers and sisters recently to ask some special questions.

Why did you start to do zazen?

How long have you been sitting?

Why did you leave Catholicism (for instance)?

And, have you had any kind of experience that is generally called mystical?

To my surprise, seven or eight out of ten say yes.

Tell me, I say. What was it?

Then he or she tells me that at such-and-such a time, under such-and-such circumstances, something happened. I ask more about it, for a clearer, more precise description. And I can't help but feel that many, many Dharma students have in fact had such an experience.

But for some reason they are disappointed. "It's disappeared." "It's not with me in my everyday life." "My everyday life now is supposed to be smooth and free and happy, comfortable...but it isn't."

This is where there is some kind of misunderstanding.

I've been doing zazen since I was twenty years old. Since the July when I was twenty-two, I have experienced what is called Realization many times, sometimes very intensely, sometimes not so. But this means that the fundamental reality, or fundamental truth of this world, or universe, or life, is as clear to me as my present understanding can reach. But as far as integration into everyday life is concerned — to be absolutely compassionate, not to be angry, to have all the other character traits that we idealize — I am far, far away from being a perfect human being.

This bothered me for a long time. But lately I see that what I used to think — what many of you think — that spiritual clarity means a perfect daily life — is just not so.

Clarity is true understanding.

Integration of that understanding into daily life, or the fusion of the two, may come with life after life of practice.

I don't know how much zazen I did in previous lives; I have no idea. I have no conscious memory but I have a feeling it was enough to walk this path in a previous life, and enough to walk this path in this life, and I hope it will be true in the next and the next and the next, life after life. In Morning Service, I silently pray, I say in my heart, life after life after life. Perhaps literally this will be endless. There will be no end.

When I came to this conclusion, that understanding by itself does not mean perfect infusion — infusion is perhaps a better word than integration — somehow I became more comfortable, easier.

In one way or another, almost all of you have experienced some understanding. Almost all of you try to deny this because you think it should be having an obvious effect on your everyday life. Although it would be ideal if our understanding were immediately usable, or evident, the fact is we have a long, long history of "greed, anger, and delusion". We are karma-beings, and that karma-being is not so easily wiped clear in one, two, ten, or twenty lives. We have lived countless lives in the past, and done countless harmful deeds.

When you have acknowledged this, look at Rinzai's point in Discourses X in the Rinzai Roku. The True Follower of the Way acts in accord with circumstances. "Circumstances" include the twentieth century, our culture and society, our individual situations in this life, and also our ancient karma-being with its accumulation of both good and bad deeds and thoughts.

How many of us can truly accept and deal with things as they come?

Rinzai says, "Accepting things as they come, he puts on his clothes. When he walks, he walks. When sits, he sits. He never has a single thought of seeking Buddhahood."

Here is an example of "accept and deal with". I used to sit all sesshin in full-lotus position. Then some time ago I broke my leg and nowadays I'm sitting half-lotus. At first I felt so guilty! So embarrassed! I thought that half-lotus was half as effective as full-lotus, logically speaking. And then one day I thought, after all this is my karma: my leg was broken. So what's wrong with sitting half-lotus? Strangely, it took me such a long time just to accept such a simple fact. A few students have to sit on chairs. What's wrong with that? Go ahead!

The true Follower of the Way will do this. When the leg hurts, he or she sits in half-lotus. When it hurts terribly, he sits on a chair. Or she alternates between chair and cushion, or between one sitting method and another. Such a simple thing.

Accept, and deal with your circumstances. Use your realizations and insights to guide you. And little by little, the karma-being will be purified.

•

You, And the Four Elements

Master Rinzai was giving a talk (Discourses XV) and someone raised a hand and asked, "What is the state in which the four elements (earth, water, fire, wind) are formless?"

Rinzai replied, "An instant of doubt in your mind and you are obstructed by earth. An instant of lust in you mind and you are drowned by water. An instant of anger in your mind and you are scorched by fire. An instant of joy in your mind and you are blown about by wind."

"An instant of doubt." About the word "doubt" I have something to say first.

In modern Zen books we often read, "With great doubt there is great enlightenment." So some kind of doubt seems to be important. But there's a problem of translation.

At Ryutaku-ji in Japan, in front of the *zendo*, there are some painted characters of Hakuin Zenji's: *Dai Gi Do*, Great Doubt Hall. The reason why Hakuin wrote this was to urge Great Doubt. But he didn't use the word the way we normally use it, in the negative sense. He used it to mean profound interest or curiosity, needing much inquiry and investigation. "What is it? Whaaat iis iit?" More questioning than doubt. Whenever you read Great Doubt, it should *not* be interpreted in the normal sense. It should be interpreted as, Whwhaat iis it? Whaaat? What *is* it? The greater the strength of that questioning, the clearer the awakening you will have. That is what's meant by doubt in the Great Doubt sense.

But in this case, Rinzai is using doubt in the ordinary sense. "An instant of doubt in your mind, and you are obstructed." Very true. "An instant of lust in your mind and you are drowned. An instant of anger in your mind and you are scorched by fire." Up to this point, there is no problem. But how about the last line: "An instant of joy in your mind and you are blown about by wind"?

The first three lines seem to make sense. Doubt, lust, and anger belong perhaps to the same negative category and must be confronted with Zen practice. But what's wrong with joy?

I think what he's saying here is, when we are so happy, so elated, we are ungrounded, unsteady. Zazen practice is grounded, and grounding.

"Gain such discernment as this" — discernment — "and you are not turned this way and that by circumstances."

You are not turned this way and that by different opinions. When A says this, I go this way. B says that, so I go that way. This quite often happens. But gain discernment and you are not turned this way and that by circumstances — nor are you stubborn!

Making use of circumstances — this is what we call Dharma activity, the virtue of zazen. Making use of circumstances. Circumstances are constantly changing. Today's are different from tomorrow's. Ever since you were born, circumstances have been changing, and most of the time you have been turned this way and that. Or stood stubbornly opposed!

"Making use of circumstances everywhere" — and then Rinzai describes very poetically the freedom of Dharma activity, which is no other than your inner activity — "you spring up in the west and sink down in the east." Or you may spring up in the north and sink down in the west! "Walking on water as you might walk on land."

No matter how many problems you have, you can carry them. Any doubt?

If you have a doubt in your mind, you are obstructed. If you have no doubt and unconditionally accept Rinzai's teaching, and Master Dogen's teaching, and sit, sit, sit, then the vital principle, or universal law, or true, true, true form of the universe, manifests itself.

"When I, a student of Dharma, look at the real form of the universe, all is the never-failing manifestation of the mysterious truth of Tathagata. In any event, in any moment, and in any place, none can be other than the marvelous revelation of its glorious light."

How is this possible? Because you have *realized* that the four elements are like a dream, like a fantasy, like bubbles, like shadows, like a flash of lightning. They don't have their own fixed entity. Then you are in "the state in which the four elements are formless."

"Followers of the Way, the You who right now is listening to my discourse is *not* your four elements. This You makes *use* of your four elements. If you can fully understand this, you are free to go or to stay as you please."

Wonderful!

•

Appreciating the Fourfold Wisdom

Now let's try to put together some of what I've been saying about Buddha Nature or Buddhadharma or essential reality, and about your own inner growth. Let's examine the koan called The Girl comes Out of Samadhi (Mumonkan, Case 42). It may seem complicated, but with a little concentration and study you will understand it.

You have probably heard of Nyogen Senzaki. He was the first Zen teacher to come to this country, and lived here for more than fifty years. He died on May 7th, 1958. In the books *Namu Dai Bosa*, and *Like A Dream, Like a Fantasy*, there is much about his life. Here is one of his prayers.

> Dharmakaya is the Buddha's holy body. It is the everlasting sea of the eternal reality of the universe. From this transcendental point of view, there is no coming of Buddha and so there is no going of Buddha. Yet, in the endless sea of phenomena arise waves of charity and lovingkindness to enlighten the ignorance of all fellow beings. The eternal reality reveals its lovingkindness in the manifestation of the waves of phenomena. Thus there is the coming of the Buddha and so there is the going of the Buddha, from the phenomenal viewpoint of life.
>
> My first prayer is that I might make of myself a mirror of Dharmakaya and reflect the whole world and all beings therein.
>
> My last prayer is that the everlasting waves will carry us all to emancipation so that we may enter the flowery garden of Buddhahood.
>
> My adoration is for the knowledge of all buddhas, and I will devote my life to the enlightenment of myself and others.

What he is saying is this. He is pointing out two aspects of reality. One aspect is *not* clearly visible. That one is: there is no coming, no going; no birth, no death; no loss, no gain. Perhaps many of you know *about* this, but only a few people have a day-to-day experience of it. That's one aspect.

The other aspect everybody knows: there is birth, there is death; there is coming, there is going. There's beginning and ending; loss and gain; purity and defilement; and there are all the other opposites. That aspect is clearly seen, perhaps too much so.

Then he said his first prayer was to make of himself a mirror, reflecting the world without making judgments, and his second prayer was to dedicate his life to the Dharma to enlighten himself and to enlighten others.

The reason why I tell you about this prayer is not only in memory of Nyogen Senzaki but because with his prayer, this koan is easier to understand.

If you are unfamiliar with Zen teisho-talks, and during a teisho I read you the text of this koan, you think you are hearing Buddhist mythology. You were brought up in a very practical world. You hear this text and it is quite different from your normal thinking.

What is the significance of a teisho? What is the relationship between zazen practice and a teisho, and what is the relationship between zazen practice and your actual life? I will try my best to answer all these questions, using this koan.

> It begins: "Manjushri Bodhisattva, the bodhisattva of wisdom, went to the assembly of the buddhas. He found that everyone had departed to his original dwelling place." Then Manjushri Bodhisattva saw that a young Dharma sister had remained and was doing zazen. She was in deep *samadhi,* close to the Buddha's seat of honor.

Let me explain a little about samadhi here and I will say more later.

There is a word in Zen tradition, *joriki*. Literally it means samadhi-energy. The energy comes out of samadhi experience.

First I must say that true Zen students will experience two things: true, clear insight or wisdom, and joriki or samadhi-energy. What I call "imperturbability" exists only when wisdom and joriki are merged. Some of us, because of our karma, can experience clear insight, true understanding, before cultivating the samadhi field or generating samadhi energy. There is another kind of student of Dharma who sits, sits, sits, cultivating this joriki, yet has no clear understanding. And there are two more categories: students who have no understanding and no samadhi experience; and of course those who have both.

You may have many misconceived ideas about zazen — that it should be without thoughts, that it should be well concentrated, that it should feel good. And these conditions do appear from time to time. But as you already know, other things such as sleepiness, pain, resistance, irritation, anger, also come from time to time. But none of this is important. The important thing is, don't give it up. Just sit. Whether it is good or bad, right or wrong, feels good, doesn't feel good, just sit, sit, sit, sit. Not only sitting after sitting, but year after year, decade after decade, so that inevitably joriki, samadhi-energy, will be well charged — the samadhi battery will be well charged. As for when you will begin to reach true understanding, *prajna*, wisdom, that cannot be predicted.

Real samadhi from the Zen point of view is this: when the wind blows, that is the wind's samadhi; when the gong rings, that is gong-samadhi; without chopsticks and without hand, that is eating-samadhi.

There is also a condition of zazen that is quite unique. It is almost impossible to describe. It's more or less like this: your body and mind are fused, without pain, without resistance, with great freedom. Somehow, fused. And yet you feel your body and mind so light. Not heavy, not dark. There is no fixed feeling such as resistance or anger; there is no such thing. You feel as if your body is empty. You are not sleeping — you are clear. Without any effort, breath comes all by itself and goes out all by itself, very rhythmically. The mind is clear.

What I have just described, with a little training almost everybody can experience. But this young Dharma sister was in a samadhi even more profound.

> So Manjushri Bodhisattva, the bodhisattva of wisdom, asked Shakyamuni Buddha, "Why can this girl sit near your seat and go into such profound samadhi while I cannot?" Shakyamuni Buddha said, "Bring her out of samadhi and ask her yourself." Manjushri Bodhisattva walked around the young woman three times and snapped his fingers.

In Buddhist tradition, this snapping of fingers has at least two meanings. One is to stimulate and to enlighten others, and the other is to purify. In Dogen Zenji's Shobogenzo, he describes how to use the bathroom. He is so kind, he even teaches how to use the bathroom. He says, whenever you enter, you should snap your fingers. Going to the bathroom is a physical purification, but Dogen sees more than this. Spiritual purification is needed also. We burn incense for the same reason. But somehow this snap! didn't work for Manjushri.

> So he "took her to Brahma heaven and exerted all his miraculous powers to bring her out of her deep samadhi, but in vain."
>
> Shakyamuni Buddha said, "Manjushri, even hundreds of thousands of Manjushris will not bring her out of her deep samadhi. But down below — past the twelve hundred million lands as innumerable as the sands of the Ganges, there is a bodhisattva called Momyo. He will be able to arouse her from her samadhi."
>
> Instantly, the bodhisattva Momyo emerged from the earth and made a bow to the World-honored One who gave him his order. The bodhisattva went to the girl and snapped his fingers. At this, she came out of samadhi.

The significant question here is pointed out in Mumon's comment on the koan. If Manjushri was such a great teacher, why couldn't he bring this girl out of samadhi? Why was Momyo, the beginner, able to do it?

Then Mumon says, "If you understand this intimately," you yourself can enter the great samadhi even "in the busiest activity of consciousness."

In the Song of Zazen, we recite, "How boundless the cleared sky of samadhi. How transparent the perfect moonlight of the fourfold wisdom...." This fourfold wisdom is a key to this koan. As you can see, there are three actors, Buddha, Manjushri Bodhisattva, and Momyo Bodhisattva, and one actress, the young Dharma sister. So four of them are acting and presenting the fourfold wisdom.

When we discuss the "fourfold wisdom", we have a tendency to grab at its meaning and hold it as information. But let us look at this from the essential or fundamental viewpoint. From here we see that each one of us has at least four different aspects. One by one, let me present them to you.

In the Heart Sutra there is the phrase, "*Fu sho, fu metsu; fu ku, fu jo; fu zo, fu gen.*" This means, "No birth, no death; no purity, no defilement; no loss, no gain." And we can add: no coming, no going; no entering, no coming out. At the beginning of our zazen practice, these sayings don't make any sense. If on the other hand someone said, "Yes, there is birth, there is death; there is loss and gain; there is entering and coming out," then everybody would understand and say, of course! This ordinary understanding is represented here by Momyo Bodhisattva.

"No birth, no death," the essential reality expressed in the Heart Sutra — that is, wisdom — is represented here by Manjushri Bodhisattva.

Because of the nature of language, nobody can express two aspects at once. So we express one aspect at one time, the other the next, and because of this presentation, we get the idea that there must be two separated aspects. This is where delusion begins, or where *dukkha* — the Sanskrit word for suffering — starts. But Shakyamuni Buddha represents both Manjushri's wisdom of no birth, no death; no coming, no going; and also Momyo's wisdom of coming and going, beginning and ending. Two aspects of one fact. Like one hand with two aspects, palm and back. So Shakyamuni Buddha represents This! — two aspects together.

Manjushri represents oneness, unity, undividedness, essential reality.

Momyo represents differentiation, "the busiest activity of consciousness," existential reality.

And the young lady who was in samadhi has the wisdom to act accordingly.

To act accordingly! When oneness-wisdom is needed, act accordingly. When differentiation-wisdom is needed, act accordingly. When Manjushri, the great teacher, speaking with the wisdom of oneness, the wisdom of the fundamental, eternal aspect, snaps his fingers, this young lady responds according to Manjushri's wisdom. She remains in a state of no birth, no death; no entering samadhi, no coming out of samadhi.

But when Momyo Bodhisattva appears, representing the wisdom of differentiation, of the phenomenal world, of impermanence, of coming and going, of entering samadhi and coming out of samadhi, she responds accordingly. She comes out of samadhi!

Now in this story, we're not talking about some young lady in the depths of samadhi. We're really talking about all these four actors' wisdom. You say, "Oh, that's nice", or "I understand." Many of you still look at this fourfold wisdom as something apart from the quintessence of your own Buddha Nature. But this is your own True Nature!

Mumon said that if you understand this intimately, you yourself can enter the great samadhi while you are living in the world of delusion. We *are* living in the world of delusion. We are living in the world of dukkha. Most of us want to escape from the world of delusion and get rid of the world of dukkha, but so far we are not successful. And we will not be successful until we can see all aspects and act accordingly.

Here is a famous koan.

Someone asked the master, "Hot and cold come. What shall I do?" The master said, "Why don't you go to the place where there is no heat, where there is no cold?"

When we hear such advice, the first thing we think about is, where is such a place on this planet? Hawaii? But even if you go to Hawaii that is not the final answer. There are cold days and extremely hot days, and we are not talking only about temperature, but about our mind, our heart, our emotional condition, our psychological condition, our physical condition, our mental condition.

So this student asked, "Where is there such a place?"
And to this, the master answered, "Sweat when it's hot. Shiver when it's cold."

Cry when you are sad, smile when you are happy.
That simple, simple action is the key point — the key point — to free ourselves from anxieties. See the fourfold wisdom intimately, and act accordingly!
There is a saying: Oneness without differentiation does not belong to Buddhadharma; differentiation without oneness does not belong to Buddhadharma. A Dharma student with some understanding can see that differentiation and oneness are two different things, like Manjushri and Momyo. But Shakyamuni Buddha in this story sees and embodies both aspects at once! If we look at this from only one side — the differentiation side — this seems to be impossible. We think these aspects must be separate; one cannot hold to two contradictory things at once.
But that idea of contradiction is the first entrance to dukkha. What we are trying to do here is gain true understanding and not be deceived by such superficial expressions as "oneness" and "differentiation". They are not at all contradictory. They harmoniously go together!
This is Shakyamuni Buddha's function in this drama. But in order for him to function he must have Manjushri's oneness, Momyo's differentiation, and the young lady acting accordingly. All these four wisdoms are necessary.

Your Buddha Nature has these four different aspects but it's only one Buddha Nature. It's only one essential, fundamental wisdom. This is what we are practicing, realizing, integrating, fusing with our daily lives. That's what zazen is for.

We are *not* just learning about Buddhist mythology.

•

Section III

Commentaries on Rinzai Zen Practice

Introduction • 83
To Do or Not To Do • 85
Ways of Teaching • 87
Who Is the Teacher? • 91
On Bowing • 93
Samadhi and Kensho • 95
Anywhere, Any Form • 99
Do Not Push Away • 101
The Value of Silence • 103
Spirit Sits • 105
At Sesshin • 107
About Koans • 109
The Dilemma of Language • 111
Marching On • 115
Why? Why? • 117
Just Mu • 119
The Realm of Mu • 121
Asking Forgiveness • 125
Redirecting Karma • 127
On Pilgrimage • 129
Renunciation • 131

Introduction

In the Rinzai Zen tradition, certain elements and forms of practice have been continued through the centuries. It's possible with the commentaries in this Section to glimpse the long history of these modes of practice and to see how our own culture is adapting them for our use.

•

To Do or Not To Do

Sometimes Master Rinzai confuses his Followers of the Way.

We already know that he found "gyo", practice, to be very important. Zazen, sesshin, chanting, the practice of awareness — these are very important. We know that he talked about the sutras and other writings as "mere displays of doctrine" or prescriptions but not the medicine itself, and he decided to put them away and do zazen.

But in the Rinzai Roku, he never discusses practice. He never says that zazen is indispensable, or that sesshin is needed. On the contrary, in Discourse XIV he uses the term "non-dependence". That is, he tells us not to depend on words, and also tells us not to depend on any specific practice, or zendo, or teacher, or sangha.

Does that mean we don't need to do zazen, or attend sesshin, or try to take part in a *kessei* (training period), or try to sharpen our awareness of every moment?

Here is a way out of this confusion.

Despite the fact that we are, as Hakuin says, "fundamentally Buddha", despite the fact that we are all right as we are, we do not think or feel that we're all right. Fear, or guilt, or greed, or discontentedness hide the fact of our Buddhahood. Therefore we start sitting to uncover that fact, to clarify it.

Master Rinzai never actually says, sit more! So why do we sit more? It is simply because unless we *do* that, we don't come to true insight. We don't clear away the fear and guilt and see our True Nature.

And then Rinzai gives us both sides at once. He says, in Discourse XVII: "It is not that I understood from the moment I was born of my mother, but that after exhaustive investigation and grinding discipline, in an instant I realized my True Nature."

This is what study and zazen and sesshin are — exhaustive investigation and grinding discipline. And where does it lead? To those instants of realization; to that recognition of non-dependence; to knowing ourselves and our True nature.

So, Followers of the Way, do study, do practice, and do realize that wonderful non-dependence of knowing Yourself.

•

Ways of Teaching

About a hundred years ago there was a very unique Zen monk in Japan. He knew everything. He had studied Buddhist philosophy and Buddhist psychology and all literatures — he was very well educated. His teacher finally said, "You are better than I am. The only thing you have to do now is go to a Zen monastery."

So, reluctantly, he went to a monastery. And because he went reluctantly, his zazen was naturally reluctant. But somehow Dharma worked in its own way. The reluctant monk became ill. He had to be separated from the other monks and was placed with a senior monk who was also ill. It was an interesting "karmic encounter". They were together in the infirmary for a couple of days and were recuperating when the senior monk said, "Excuse me, but I understand you know everything. This is a good chance for me to hear your lecture on the Heart Sutra."

The reluctant monk said, "Of course. That would be very easy for me."

So the two monks, still recuperating, sat and faced each other and the reluctant monk began to lecture on the Heart Sutra beginning with *"Kan ji zai bo sa..."* and explaining as he went. He came to *shiki soku ze ku, ku soku ze shiki..."* — form is no other than shunyata, shunyata is no other than form" — and he was explaining what shunyata is and what form and formlessness are, and so on.

The senior monk said, "Wait!" He pointed to his fan and said, "Is this form? Is this formlessness?"

The reluctant monk said immediately, "Of course this is form."

The senior monk said, "Okay, I have the form aspect. Now give me the formlessness aspect."

Whereupon, this most intelligent monk could not say even a word.

Then the senior monk said, "There are two kinds of Zen teaching. One is called *Soshi* Zen and the other is *Nyorai* Zen."

Then he must have said further that Nyorai Zen is the more verbal, intellectual understanding of Buddhadharma while Soshi Zen uses no explanation — just presentation! "You know Nyorai Zen very well. Now you must learn to present Soshi Zen."

Here is a story from the Rinzai Roku, Critical Examinations, XXIII.

> Five hundred monks were assembled at Kinzan but few asked Kinzan for instruction. Obaku ordered Rinzai to go to Kinzan. Then he asked, "What will you do when you get there?"
> "When I get there, I'll know what to do," said Rinzai.
> Rinzai arrived at Kinzan. Still wearing his traveling clothes, he went to the Dharma Hall to see the Master of Kinzan. Just as the Master raised his head, Rinzai shouted, and when the Master started to open his mouth, Rinzai swung his sleeves as he turned and left.
> Shortly after, a monk asked the Master of Kinzan, "What did you say just now that made that monk shout at you?"
> He replied, "That monk came from Obaku's assembly. If you want to know, ask him."
> Of the five hundred monks at Kinzan, most departed to taste Soshi Zen.

This is Rinzai's vivid Soshi Zen. He shouted! He swung his sleeves and left the Dharma Hall. If on the other hand I explain something to you about the concept of karma, that may be called Nyorai Zen — intellectually understandable. "If you want to know, ask him" is typical Nyorai Zen.

We cannot say which is better; we need both. Yasutani Roshi was an excellent Nyorai Zen teacher. Soen Roshi was a typical Soshi Zen master.

Five hundred monks were assembled but few did zazen. This was a Zen monastery, supposedly a zazen training center, but many of the monks didn't do zazen. So the Master worried and worried. Finally he sent a messenger to consult Huang Po — Obaku Kiun Zenji. Obaku asked his head monk, Rinzai, to go and see whether he could help with the situation at Kinzan. Just before Rinzai departed, Obaku asked, "What will you do when you get there?" This is a very natural question. And Rinzai replied, "When I get there, I will know what to do." This is a very wonderful statement.

You know, I come every day during sesshin to give teisho and I prepare and prepare. But until I sit down and sip this orange juice, my mind is blank, like white paper. I'm not prepared to say the first sentence. Seeing your faces, somehow it comes. "When I get there, I will know what to do."

Rinzai arrived at Kinzan with what I call "hara sense", and still wearing his travelling clothes, went to the Dharma Hall to see the Master. And just as the Master raised his head to greet Rinzai, Rinzai shoouuted!! and "swung his sleeves and left!"

Shortly after, a monk asked the Master, "What did you say just now that made that monk shout at you?" Kinzan replied, "That monk came from Obaku. If you want to know, ask him."

No wonder five hundred monks did not do zazen. "If you want to know, ask him."

"Of the five hundred monks, most departed to taste Soshi Zen."

By Rinzai's one shout, one *Kwaaaatz!*, he purified Kinzan monastery. This is called Soshi Zen. This naturally requires clear insight and confidence in samadhi-energy, in joriki. Dynamic clarity, from steady, steady, day-by-day sitting. And it requires a mysterious confidence. This confidence makes this thing possible.

All the "Critical Examinations", or Mutual Examinations, recorded in the Rinzai Roku are Soshi Zen stories.

Vital Zen.

•

Who Is the Teacher?

Obaku Kiun Zenji said, in the Hekiganroku, Case 11, "Don't you know that in all the land of Tang there is no Zen teacher?"

Many of you came here thinking there was a Zen teacher, a Zen master. "He might solve all my problems. He might help me. I can depend on him, rely on him. He must be kind, generous...." NO, no, no, that is a misconception. If you think that way, drop it right now. Obaku wants you to be independent.

Obaku is kind. He said, "Don't you know there is no Zen teacher?" Then someone stood up and said, "But what about Zen groups in New York City? in Rochester? in San Francisco? And what about the Tibetans? and gurus and swamis and rinpoches?" Obaku said, "I did not say there is no Zen anywhere in China." I did not say there is no Zen anywhere in the universe. In fact, the universe is filled. There is nothing else but This Matter!

But there is no teacher, as such, for you to rely on but yourself. Yourself.

This is a unique part of the Zen tradition. In some other traditions it may be said that someone teaches something to the student. The teacher passes on some material knowledge or accumulation of knowledge and the student thinks, "Oh I *learned* something from this person." But from the essential viewpoint, there is no giver, no receiver, no donation. The giver is shunyata, the receiver is shunyata, the donation is shunyata. Teaching is *also* shunyata. To realize this by your own effort is called Zen practice and Zen realization.

Now here is a subtle point. It is said that sutra-reading is unimportant. But it says that in the sutras. Unless you study the sutras, you will not understand the insignificance of studying the sutras. It is this way with a Zen teacher. Unless you have studied with a teacher, you will not understand the importance of depending upon yourself. So you should do both: you should study with a teacher;

and you should recognize the limited role of the teacher. You are the student, and you are the teacher.

The practice of zazen — the practice of anything — is lonely. It's really lonely. Unless you can endure this loneliness, unless you can establish an intimate relationship with yourself, your *essential* self, you will not attain deep realization.

•

On Bowing

Each one of you has some kind of status or position or situation in life. Many of you think that through your own efforts you got to that position. But that's not the correct way of looking at it according to Mahayana Buddhism. You need to recognize that there is a Something. I have given you many names for it: Buddha Nature, Ultimate Reality, Shunyata, Mu or, as Soen Roshi called it, Endless Dimension Universal Life. Because of this Universal Life, we do our work and have a position. To this Universal Life, we bow. We bow. This is Universal Life bowing to Universal Life. This is Buddha Nature bowing to Buddha Nature. This is Mu bowing to Mu.

Zazen is another form of bowing.

•

Samadhi and Kensho

Let me speak again about samadhi.

We go into and come out of samadhi. When we go into it deeply, everything disappears. The self disappears; surroundings disappear. A natural question is, "How do you know the self disappears if the self disappears?" This seems to be a reasonable question, but once we enter samadhi we find that the question itself is unnecessary. Even the question disappears. Even the expectation of any brilliant answer disappears.

The word "disappearance" may sound negative but that is just a connection we make to certain words. To put it simply, in that vital condition of samadhi, not a thing exists. This is kensho: seeing the true form of the universe.

But most of the time we live separated from this condition, thinking that I am here and you are there and that mountain is over there. Because of this misunderstanding, that the self as such has its own existence, there come all the problems and all the suffering that we experience in human life.

Both samadhi and kensho are essential to living. Yasutani Roshi used this illustration: Samadhi is the gasoline that makes the car move, that gives us energy for life; kensho is the headlighting without which we quickly lose our way.

We say in The Four Vows, *"Shujo muhen seigando"*, "However innumerable all beings are, I vow to save them all," or, to liberate them all, including myself. The real meaning of "save" is to experience samadhi. That condition — no thing, not a thing — is what Joshu called Mu, or it is called Buddha Nature, or God, or Tao, or Ultimate Reality, or The Something, or Kami by Japanese Shintoists.

When we have experienced that vital condition, no theology and no philosophy are necessary. A person who has not had that vital experience, and who needs to talk *about* it, needs theology and philosophy for explanation and communication. We do not gather together in sesshin for theoretical discussion but for each one of us to taste that most positive Nothingness that is our true nature.

We say, "All beings are fundamentally Buddha," but until we go into that most positive Nothingness condition called samadhi, we are unable to believe that all beings are fundamentally Buddha. And more importantly, until we experience that most positive Nothingness, we are unable to be liberated from many, many kinds of suffering. For this reason zazen practice, intense concentration on Mu, is so vital.

For many people — for Shakyamuni Buddha, for the patriarchs — simply going into that condition profoundly, and coming out and going in, is all that is necessary, the more often the better. For them, the systematized koan study we have inherited from Hakuin Zenji is not necessary.

We all agree that life is full of wonderful things as well as problems and sufferings. We agree that we would like to be free from the sufferings spoken of in the Four Noble Truths and the Eightfold Path of the Buddhist tradition. The cause of suffering is a misunderstanding about the existence of self. The truth is, as is said in the Diamond Sutra, the self is like a dream, a phantasm, a bubble and a shadow, a dewdrop and a flash of lightning. This self is a temporary appearance or temporary condition. The fundamental condition is Positive Nothingness, or Mu. We must experience this in samadhi.

There are two ways to look at the practice of Mu. You may say that the practice of Mu is to cut off, or to break through, preconceived ideas and notions. Or, you may say that the practice of Mu is simply to realize that we are, from the beginning, Mu, or shunyata, or Positive Nothingness.

"All beings are fundamentally Buddha" when seen from an enlightened viewpoint. But so far we are all bumpkins. And so we strive, strive, Mu, Mu, to enter the condition of Positive Nothingness, the "true form of the universe", the place where we no longer need to strive and indeed cannot strive. Making use of this temporary formation, this body — that is, in this life doing Mu with vitality — we realize the fundamental, no-form, Positive Nothingness.

What I'm telling you now is not information acquired from reading books or hearing lectures. What I'm saying to you is what I learned myself by entering that samadhi condition. Going into it, coming out of it, going into it, coming out of it. Once you taste it you cannot forget it. Your way of thinking changes one hundred and eighty degrees. This change in "upside-down views" is called *do* — *"Shujo muhen seigan do"* — or, freeing and being freed.

As long as we have a physical body there are many sufferings that accompany us, but once this upside-down view is rightside-up then, as the Heart Sutra says, "at last, nirvana." It is essential for each one of you to enter this Mu Positive Nothingness samadhi.

•

Anywhere, Any Form

Let me tell a story Soen Roshi loved to tell during teishos.

There was a Japanese Zen master who lived about a hundred years ago. One of his lay students lost her grandchild and because of her sadness, she became ill. Her family informed her Zen teacher. One day, he visited her in the hospital, perhaps bringing a flower, and inquired how she was getting along. She was in bed, crying, crying. The Zen master said, "Would you like to see your grandchild again?"

Half hopeful, she asked him, "I would very much like to see my beloved granddaughter again, but tell me how?"

He said, "You're in bed, not doing anything, and therefore you can do the Nembutsu. Just say '*Namu Amida Butsu, Namu Amida Butsu*' all day long and I will come and see you again next week." He left, and as she was so desperate to see her delicious, sweet daughter's daughter she began chanting, chanting, chanting. Of course doubts, such as you have during zazen, visited her quite often. But still she continued, continued all day long and the next day and the following day. One week passed.

The Zen master came to visit her again and she was doing Namu Amida Butsu. He thought, "She's doing very well" and he knocked on the door and entered her room. "How's everything?"

"Ever since you told me to, I've been doing the Nembutsu but my granddaughter doesn't come back."

"All right. One more week."

He came back again. "How is it?"

She said, "I enjoy the Nembutsu very much but I have a problem. Because I've had to chant Namu Amida Butsu for two weeks, my mouth is exhausted. Is there any better, easier way than this?"

He said, "All right, there is."

There was a ticking alarm clock. "Can you hear that? Do nothing but listen to the sound of that alarm clock." He left.

She followed his instructions and when he came back a week later, her concentration had increased. He felt the readiness of time was nearing. A week or two later when he visited her, her face was full of joy!

With tears she said to him, "Thank you so much. Now I understand what you mean by saying I can see my beloved granddaughter again."

That is the end of the story. Soen Roshi adds that zazen can be done any place, in any form, and self-realization is possible. Through this self-realization, one can truly see this deathlessness and birthlessness.

•

Do Not Push Away

The Engaku Sutra says, "When you do zazen, do not search for the Pure Land. When you sit, do not seek for enlightenment. Do not try to push away the world of defilement. If you have delusions, do not try to extinguish them."

It sounds very easy to do this: when you sit, do not search, do not strive, do not try, do not push away, do not extinguish. "Pushing away" or "extinguishing delusions" sounds comprehensible and possible, but in fact it is deceptive and impossible. "Do not push away" sounds impossible, but it is *essentially* true.

"But realize" — *realize* is the key word — "realize that delusion is no other than the manifestation of Mu." The world of defilement is *also* no other than Mu. Endless thoughts are no other than the manifestation of Mu. Realize that. Realize This!

We tend to think that thoughts are bad, that the world of defilement is poison, and delusions are not good. Therefore we push them away by searching for enlightenment or the Pure Land. Instead, realize who you are, what you are, so that both defilement and purity are seen to be none other than Mu itself. Birth, death, pain, fear, are all Mu itself. And Mu is, as you know, just a syllable for something which cannot be spoken, which is unnameable, which is It.

"Do not say: cold is cold; hot is hot." This is just description. Do not describe *about* Mu. Rather, realize Mu, live Mu, express Mu directly — not "about". This is not a matter of metaphysical definition. When we go into metaphysics, I get such a headache!

•

The Value of Silence

> Vimalakirti asked Manjushri Bodhisattva, "What is the non-dualistic Dharma gate through which the bodhisattvas pass?"
> Manjushri replied, "According to my understanding, it is non-talking, non-preaching, non-suggestion, non-recognition, transcending all dialogue. This is called the non-dualistic Dharma gate."

Manjushri said, "According to my understanding...." According to his experiential understanding. After all, This Matter cannot be talked of, cannot be discussed, cannot be preached.

When Manjushri asked Vimalakirti, "What is your opinion?" Vimalakirti sat in Great Silence.

There is an interesting story about a "thunderous silence".

A Zen priest in Tokyo was asked to be a marriage consultant. One day, a middle-aged man and woman, husband and wife, came to him. First he heard the opinion of the wife and it made great sense to him. He thought, "No wonder she wants to divorce him." And then he listened to the husband's opinion against the divorce and thought it made absolute sense. The priest wanted to sustain the marriage, but how could he do this? So he sat thinking, thinking, in *great* silence.

The husband and wife, watching the priest's suffering, began to talk to each other. "Look," they said, "he is suffering for us. There's no reason for him to suffer for us. If you and I understand each other, there's no problem." They agreed: you're right; all right. And after about ten minutes or so of the priest's suffering and silence, they solved the problem by themselves.

Now this is perhaps too Oriental for you. But this kind of thing happens. Sometimes the less talk the better.

There is a similar story about Ryokan. He was a famous poet and calligrapher, very transcendent, very great, one of the greatest in Japanese history. He had a nephew who was really terrible — beyond the parents' control. Whatever they said, the nephew wouldn't listen. So the parents finally asked Ryokan to say something so the nephew might change.

Ryokan reluctantly spent the night at his brother's. They expected Ryokan to talk to the nephew and say, do this, don't do that, don't, don't, but Ryokan didn't do anything at all. The nephew was more or less expecting to hear some bitter advice from his uncle but Uncle Ryokan didn't say *anything*.

The following morning, Ryokan was leaving without even saying a word. The nephew came and saw Ryokan shed one tear. One teardrop.

That silent tear changed this uncontrollable, wild, uncouth nephew, with a snap! This kind of thing happens once in a while. Usually, the more we say without sufficient virtue in ourselves, the more the resistance by nephew or niece or son or daughter or friend.

So this is Vimalakirti's Great Silence, and Ryokan's silence with a teardrop, and the Tokyo priest's silence with a headache. I see this as an Oriental approach, while in the West the approach may be slightly different — spelling out this and this and this. It might work and it might not. Great Silence might work and it might not. But it's good for you to know there is this kind of teaching. Silent teaching.

Many, many, bodhisattvas spoke about the non-dualistic Dharma gate.

> Then Manjushri said to Vimalakirti, "All of us have spoken. Please tell us what a bodhisattva's initiation into the non-dual Dharma is." Vimalakirti kept silent.
>
> Then Manjushri said, "Excellent! Excellent! Can there be true initiation into the non-dual Dharma before word and speech are no longer written or spoken?"

It's important for us to know silence.

•

Spirit Sits

The Vimalakirti Sutra is one of the most important Mahayana Buddhist texts through which the essence of Mahayana and Zen Buddhism is expressed. The sutra tells a long story and I will just present one small part of it. There are at least three different translations available of the Vimalakirti Sutra. I recommend that you spend two or three days, at least, in reading this sutra. I will just give you the flavor of it.

Vi, in Sanskrit, means to depart, to be away. *Mala* means defilement. So *vimala* means to wash or to be clean, or to be away from defilement, both mental and spiritual.

There was a lay person named Vimalakirti who was quite rich and generous, with deep understanding of This Matter. He lived somewhere in India.

As an *upaya*, or "skillful means" (of teaching), he became sick, and many friends inquired about his condition. He was hoping that Shakyamuni Buddha would come to visit him but instead, Shakyamuni Buddha tried to send his disciples, one by one. However, there was always a good reason why each one would not go.

The first student whom Shakyamuni Buddha wanted to send to inquire after the health of Vimalakirti was Shariputra. But Shariputra said, "Oh no, no, please! I'm your student and I know I should be obedient but in this case, please excuse me!" So Shakymuni Buddha said, "Why?"

Well, it seems that Shariputra had met Vimalakirti some years before and had been completely overcome in argument. They were talking about zazen. Shariputra had his own ideas about what zazen should be and he expressed his ideas to Vimalakirti.

Vimalakirti said, "Wrong. No. Your understanding of zazen is incorrect." And then he began to teach, to tell Shariputra about zazen using his own experience and wide, profound knowledge.

The essence of it was this: when you do zazen, you and breath sit. Or, breath sits. Breath sits, rather than you, sitting and breathing.

This reminds me of an interesting story about Dokyo Etan Zenji — a name we chant in our lineage list — the teacher of Hakuin Zenji. He was living in a small temple in Nagano Prefecture and in those days there were many wolves. They came out of the forest and ate pigs, cows, and sometimes human babies. So the village people came to ask, "Master, can you do something?" Dokyo Zenji said, "All right. Where do you see the wolves?"

"They appear in the cemetery about midnight."

So Dokyo Zenji went to the cemetery and did zazen. About midnight, many wolves appeared. One leaped over his head and one sniffed around him. You know if this were to happen to us, our hearts would be beating rapidly and we would be showing fear, and probably we would be attacked immediately. But what Dokyo Etan Zenji did was breath-sit. I like this: breath-sat. The wolves jumped and touched and smelled — very nice food for them to eat, no defense, no protection, but *deep* zazen, *deep* breath, and they could not attack Dokyo Etan Zenji. From the next day on, they all disappeared.

"As for zazen in the Mahayana, we have no words to praise it fully."

So to repeat, along with Shariputra many of us have the idea that some kind of material body does some kind of spiritual practice. But this idea is a great impediment to practice. You know the connection between the words "breath" and "spirit" in Latin. It is the spirit that fills the body, not the body that does spiritual practice.

So Shariputra, still struggling to change his ideas about zazen, was very reluctant to visit Vimalakirti and he asked the Buddha please to send someone else.

•

At Sesshin

Here is some practical advice about zazen.

Today is the fifth day of sesshin. For some of you, the legs may be very painful but for most of you, your zazen is very clear. However, we are all a little tired. We think we need some kind of intermission. But if we do that, then tomorrow we have to begin from the beginning. So even though it's very hard, we do seven days without intermission.

Today it's raining. It is said that listening to the rain or to insects or to other natural sounds is very helpful for us to enter deep samadhi. The sesshin leader and I will encourage you but your own encouragement is more effective. Just keep doing. This is a very simple sentence, but I repeat: just keep doing. Such a short sentence is normally not worth paying attention to. It's not particularly exciting, or profound. But at this point on the fifth day of sesshin, it is the best advice I can give you. Just keep doing.

•

About Koans

Etymologically speaking, "ko-an" means a place and a time where the truth is.

Regardless of the title of a koan, or who is speaking, or what the events are, or what the setting is, we are always dealing with Buddha Nature. Our koan is Buddha Nature.

As we know, there is no time, no place, that is not the truth. From morning to night we are working on the *genjo koan*, the everyday-life koan.

The koans most familiar to us come from the Mumonkan, The Gateless Gate collection, or from the Hekiganroku, the Blue Cliff Collection. There are several English translations of these two and there are many other collections as well. The Book of Equanimity, for instance, or The Iron Flute, koans collected and edited by Nyogen Senzaki and Ruth McCandless. There is a collection of my own choices, with Western additions, for American Zen students. Some modern masters, like the teachers in ancient times, make up their own koans spontaneously as they try to awaken the student to fundamental Buddha Nature. Sooner or later these too will be collected.

•

The Dilemma of Language

In the Mumonkan, Case 48, Kempo's One Way, a monk said to Master Kempo, "It is written, 'Bhagavats in the ten directions. One straight road to nirvana.' I still wonder where the road can be." Kempo lifted his staff, drew a line, and said, "Here it is."

The word *bhagavat* has at least six different meanings and translations but in this case, take it as "buddha". The buddhas in the ten directions have one way to nirvana. "I wonder where that one way is."

Here again, the problem of language. No matter how often we say that we mean absolute oneness, that we are not using the language of duality, nevertheless, if we read "one way to nirvana" we cannot help but think there is one way, and there is nirvana. If we take that one way, we will reach nirvana someday.

At the heart of our zazen practice is this problem of language. Because of the nature of language, Mu-practice will give you the impression that if a student is doing Mu, and if Mu is done sufficiently, and the readiness of time comes, then there is kensho, enlightenment, waiting for the student. This is the impression you might get from hearing about Mu-practice.

On the other hand, hearing about *shikantaza*, just sitting, you get the impression that this very sitting is none other than the manifestation of Buddha Nature, "this very body is the body of the Buddha, this very place is the Lotus Land of Purity."

Now the problem is, we can memorize this line of poetry and do zazen and say, "This very being is the being of the Buddha and this very cushion is the cushion of Pure Land," but to *feel* so, or believe so, is another story. Only with struggle, and practice, practice, practice, one day — not, one of these days, but *one* day, ONE DAY, always Today! — we will come to realization.

Indeed, this very place *is* the Lotus Land of Purity. But that is not to say, "This is nice, but the Deluded World of Defilements is not nice." This very place is the Deluded World of Defilements! The Deluded World and the Lotus Land are identical, *essentially* speaking.

"This very body is the body of a bumpkin" but that's not very encouraging. "This very body is the body of the Buddha" — that's partly encouragement and partly deception. If our Dharma eye is open, we will not be disturbed by chanting, "This very body is the body of the bumpkin" or, "This very street is Skid Row." It's understandable to feel reluctant to chant this but *essentially* we must not be deceived by beautiful expressions.

In the same way, "Bhagavats in the ten directions have only one way to nirvana" is very deceptive.

> "I wonder where that one way is."
> Kempo lifted his staff and drew a line and said, "Here it is."

What does this mean? This is very important.

"Bhagavats in the ten directions have only one way to nirvana" is more or less equivalent to "Buddha Nature pervades the whole universe, revealing right here now." It's a beautiful expression and everybody likes it. But the point is, how much does our breathing, for instance, pervade the whole universe? How often do we feel this? "Buddha Nature pervades the whole universe, revealing right here now" is not just a poetic expression. Each of us has the task, "moment after moment", breath after breath, to see this.

How well can we transcend the borderlines between so-called past and present and so-called future? How well can we erase those borderlines? How well can we erase the borderline between so-called here and so-called there, between samsara and nirvana? How well can we erase these lines which in truth don't exist, and yet which exist as concepts? "I wonder where that one way is." This is one: no past, no future, but *one* day. This is one: no this, no that, but This!

Later, the same monk asked Ummon Bunen Zenji the same question. Ummon held up his fan and said, "This fan jumps up to the thirty-third heaven and hits the nose of the deity there. When a carp of the eastern sea is struck with a stick, the rain comes down in torrents."

This part is very confusing for beginners but this is the part Soen Roshi loved. He gave this teisho many times, especially this second part. He was not like me; I explain too much, which isn't good. When it came to this part, he opened up his fan and hit his own nose!

At this point it is not necessary for you to understand every word, but it is necessary for you to understand the nature of Buddha Nature. It functions mysteriously. Ummon is saying that some nen, some thoughts, some actions, transmit energy by themselves. Do you know the toy that has three strings with three spheres hanging from them? The right ball hits the center one which never moves, but the left ball swings out. The power, or energy, goes through the center ball which behaves as though nothing happened. This is how Buddha Nature or karma works, although it's not as simple to observe. Some action takes place *here* and completely different things happen *there*. But all these are none other than the function or activity of Buddha Nature.

Mumon comments in his verse on Master Kempo's One Way: "Before a step is taken, the goal is reached."

Normally we say, "Unless a step is taken, the goal will not be reached." But in this verse Mumon goes on to say, "Before the tongue is moved, the speech is finished."

There *is* such an aspect, such a world. Here is our eternal dilemma. Existential reality requires language. Fundamental reality, which does not require language at all, sometimes has to be explained, and by language which belongs to the category of existential reality.

So you understand why we say, Mu. Just Mu.

If you prefer, I can give you a beautiful talk, but so what? We'll end up with all kinds of deceptive ideas. At least you should understand right now that there is only one thing for you to do — that is, Mu. And Mu will take care of it. That's all I can say. *Butsu do mujo seiganjo.* "However endless the Buddha's Way is, we vow to contine," to march on.

•

Marching On

In the koan collection Mumonkan, The Gateless Gate, Case 46, the question is asked: "How can you proceed on further from the top of a hundred-foot pole?"

Or, "You who sits on the top of a hundred-foot pole, although you have entered the Way, you are not yet fully enlightened. You must proceed on from the top of the pole and manifest your whole body in the ten directions."

This is a typical Zen koan. It seems designed to confuse you. You might think this is the story of a circus, with a hundred-foot pole held perpendicularly and you are sitting on top of it. But that's not the case.

Once in a while during zazen, you experience what you may call "a high", or something "deep". But "...you are not yet fully enlightened." You are not there yet. Soen Roshi often said to me, not yet, not yet. And I say to you, march on, march on.

It's as true in the East as in the West that we are goal-oriented. For us, "not yet" and "march on" are not what we want to hear. We prefer to hear "pretty soon" or "you got it".

And if you "got it", so what? What next? The universe is boundless — "...how boundless, the cleared sky of samadhi..." — endless. *Therefore* not yet, march on. Looking back, there was a time when I thought I had clear insight, but nowadays I feel it is not yet.

"Proceed on from the top of the pole and you will manifest your whole body in the ten directions."

Now this is the trickiness of language again. In one way, it sounds as if you must manifest your own body in all the ten directions. But at the same time, this is an affirmative statement that whether we're aware of it or not, we are manifesting our own beings — in the ten directions, eleven directions, twenty-five directions. The translator has a problem: English precision; Chinese ambiguity. The translator must choose between two correct sentences: "You must manifest" and "Your being is already manifesting." I cannot write both sentences. It would be easier if one sentence could imply the two possibilities, essential nature and existential nature. When I translate from Chinese to English, I confront the problem each time. Should I focus on the essential nature or on the existential nature? And once it is translated into one or the other, you read the sentence as one hundred percent of the truth in spite of the fact that it's only fifty percent of the truth.

So in one sense, you must manifest your whole body in the ten directions. In another sense, there's no need to proceed on from the top of the pole. Whether you like it or not, your body is already manifesting in the ten directions.

Then some of you may ask, "That being the case, why do we have to do zazen?"

My answer is this. Until your realization comes to the point where you see that your being — the gong's being, the microphone's being, today's beautiful weather, yesterday's wet weather, all kinds of Buddha-Nature phenomena — are in *fact* nothing but manifestations of This Matter, you must work. To realize, to manifest. That's why we're doing Mu, mu, mu, mu, mu.

•

Why? Why?

Rinzai came to Mount Obaku in the middle of the summer training period. He stayed a few days and then tried to take his leave.

Obaku said, "You came in violation of the rules of the summer kessei and now you're leaving before it's over."

"I came for a little while to pay my respects to you," said Rinzai.

Obaku hit him and chased him out.

After he had gone a few miles, Rinzai, thinking the matter over, returned to the temple and finished the summer training period.

Rinzai stayed a few days, then tried to leave.

"You came in violation of the rules of the training period and now you're leaving before it's over."

To say "I came for a little while to pay my respects to you" sounds polite, but going and coming just shows Rinzai's confusion to Obaku. It was not the best greeting from Obaku's point of view. He is concerned for Rinzai, he cares, he is kind. So the greeting, "I come to pay my respects" is not important. What is important is that you, and Rinzai, either participate or don't come.

Obaku struck Rinzai and chased him out.

Now this is a key point. After he had gone a few miles, Rinzai thought this over. *Why* did he hit me? *Why* did he kick me out? *Why* did he hit me? *Why* did he kick me out? These are not personal matters. There must be something much deeper. Why?

This deep questioning is your state of mind when working with a koan.

Rinzai decided to find out Why? so he returned to the temple and finished the kessei.

Many, many centuries later, one patriarch commented on this. He said that the reason why Rinzai Zen is still alive, still has life and an uninterrupted Dharma lineage, is simply because of Rinzai's "thinking the matter over" and returning to the temple.

•

Just Mu

"Just sit" or "just Mu" are phrases that are not well understood. "Just Mu" is not "Oh, today my Mu is good, my sitting is good." That's not "just Mu". That's judgmental Mu.

To say "just Mu" is easy, but to do "just Mu" is *so* difficult.

•

The Realm of Mu

At Ryutaku-ji in Japan, there is a calligraphy of Gempo Roshi's — "In the myriad forms, a single body is revealed." *"Banzo shichu doku ro shin."* He told us why he liked those words particularly.

Yamamoto Gempo Roshi did not have a formal education. He became a monk at about the age of twenty-five and he traveled to many different Zen monasteries. In one of these, he was given the koan "Joshu's Mu", Mumonkan, Case 1. So, like you, he sat with Mu. Mu, mu, mu, mu, day after night and day after day and night after night. Whether he did MU! forcefully or whether he did mu ceaselessly, I don't know. Perhaps you know by now, when we get into it, it does it all by itself. It is not: I do Mu.

And then one day a priest came to visit the monastery and he was wearing colorful robes. Something about the sunshine on the colorful robes, shining or glittering or literally illuminating, enabled Yamamoto to pass through the Gateless Gate.

Later, under Kyuho Roshi, Yamamoto was assigned the Myriad Forms koan from the Book of Equanimity, Case 64, "Shisho's Transmission". The student Gempo-to-be sat and sat and then presented his insight to Roshi. It was refused. He sat, sat, presented, presented; it was rejected, rejected. This continued for 365 days. He may have gone to dokusan a hundred times with different presentations. "No, no, no." *Ching, ching* went the bell.

Then one day student-Gempo presented something and Roshi rang his little bell, and when his student bowed, Kyuho Roshi hit him hard with an archery bow he'd been hiding. Gempo Roshi said he was hit so hard he couldn't move for three days, but he had suddenly understood Myriad Forms.

For the rest of his life he was really grateful for this one year and this hidden archery bow. Whenever he talked about it, he talked with tears. And so he did the calligraphy.

Perhaps surprisingly, Gempo Roshi did not succeed to Kyuho Roshi's Dharma. He studied under six or seven different teachers.

He had a great thirst for mastering This Matter. Eventually he studied with Shounshitsu Sohan Gempo Roshi and became his Dharma heir, taking one of his names. So his first kensho with Mu was with one roshi; his deep kensho with Myriad Forms was with another; and yet he became the Dharma heir of Sohan Gempo Roshi. This mysterious karmic activity is inconceivable and inexpressible.

What did he get? *What* did he get? What do we get? What did he get with Mu? What did he get with Myriad Forms?

Many years ago I was talking with Huston Smith, the scholar and teacher who wrote "The Religions of Man" and other books. We were talking about transmission and he kept asking, "Transmit what?" Now, he knew that the robe and the bowl and other objects that a teacher presents to a student are just symbols. So he deeply wanted to know, "Transmit what?"

You may have the impression that there is some required course to finish. But it is really more like this: When so-called teacher and so-called student can enter the realm of Mu, then there is transmission.

We are always in the midst of Mu without realizing it. But I mean, to enter the realm of Mu with lucid realization. When two mirrors face each other, there is infinite reflection. But when there is no space between the mirrors, there is no reflection. Therefore, infinity. At a certain time, at a certain point, something mysterious like this will happen.

Normally in Rinzai tradition, there is first kensho, then koan study. But then there is also what I call "skinship", or kinship of the spirit, or a relationship of empathy between teacher and student for many years. Then at last teacher and student enter the realm of Mu. Nothing to say, nothing to hear, nothing to give, nothing to receive, nothing to transmit! That is Transmission Day.

Now, do not think this is someone else's story. During sesshin, for instance, you are sitting me, I am sitting you. There is nothing to teach, nothing to give, nothing to receive. There is no one to give. And there is no one to receive.

This is where language is so limited. This is really where words end, and this is the very point where Zen begins. It's the very point where we simply sit down and do Mu.

There is an expression: "Donor is shunyata; receiver is shunyata; donation is shunyata." If shunyata is Emptiness, or Formlessness, this doesn't sound like a lot to receive. But in fact, because of the limitlessness of This, what you receive is much more than "the three hundred galaxies of gold and silver."

To summarize, our traditional system is certainly different from any school system or any kind of credit system or any kind of degree system. No certificates. It's on a different level, or in a different dimension. Unless you shift your habitual thought, it's rather difficult for you to go into the "realm of Mu".

The point is, what we do in zazen — the realm we go into — has nothing to do with degrees or grades or certificates. All we have to do is fade away, or vanish, or melt into.... At first, we're afraid. We're afraid to lose our identity. We are afraid and curious at the same time. Curious to go into the new realm, but afraid of it. We go very close to the borderline but then we say "Wait..," and we back off. And it takes a long time just to come close to the border. Then it's one more step but somehow we step back. "An instant of doubt." Fear. Fear.

But if we repeat this again and again and again, by doing zazen, by attending sesshins, we become used to it. Even hell, I assume, if we visit it many times, is not as awful as it sounds. And heaven, not so impressive.

So we go on, afraid. Repeat, repeat, repeat, repeat. And one day, we enter that special realm of Mu. This is where kensho takes place, where the transmission of Dharma takes place. Head Monk Shisho said to Hogen, "Today is a very important day."

And *today* is a very important day. For what? For transmission? For learning to manage your pain? To manage your fear and resistance? To accept your own karma instead of hating it? Today. Whenever it takes place. Today. Today is very important for you.

"*Banzo shichu doku ro shin.*" Even if you don't read Chinese, this is very rhythmic and forceful. "In the myriad forms, a single body is revealed." This is what Yamamoto Gempo Roshi struggled with — struggled, struggled. "Buddha Nature pervades the whole universe, revealing right here now" sounds very much the same thing, doesn't it? Even that great Zen master Gempo Roshi took a year to pass this koan.

Please don't be discouraged.

•

Asking Forgiveness

Here is something important.

We have a painful leg. We are lucky to have a painful leg, or sleepy mind, or stiff shoulder, or low bloodpressure. All these bodily things, we still have because so-called death has not yet come to us. While we are living we can practice Mu for self-realization, and also — this is very important — also to purify our karma.

One morning when Gempo Roshi was over ninety years old, he said to Soen Roshi, "Yesterday Mr. X came to see me and I said something that might have hurt him. So last night at midnight, I woke up and sat down on the floor facing Mr. X's house and bowed and apologized. 'I'm terribly sorry for what I said. Please, please forgive me.' "

This kind of pleeease! has strong nen energy. While we are still alive, able to think, able to feel, sense, express, using this living body we ask, "Please excuse me! Please pardon me!"

In the Morning Service we chant the Purification, or Confession. While we are living in our body the most essential thing we do is zazen. But we also use thinking, feeling, sensing, and every occasion to say, *please* pardon me.

In this way we also help to purify the karma.

•

Redirecting Karma

To experience insight, to come to know realization, is difficult. The physical part is not too difficult. The emotional and psychological parts are a little more difficult. But the karmic part — that's the most difficult. The greatest impediment is karma.

Torei Enji Zenji said — and I expand on what he said — there are three things to do to purify or beautify or redirect our karma.

Number one is to bow fully. We do a few bows a day but he means many, many bows throughout our life, not as exercise, but beautifully as in yoga.

Number two is to do zazen.

Number three is to say and feel the Purification or Confession verse from Morning Service, to ask over and over for forgiveness, and for understanding and compassion. To ask from our hearts.

It's not the physical aspect of zazen that is difficult. It doesn't matter whether you sit on a cushion or a chair or a bench, or two-and-a-half cushions. Whether your back is straight or not is not so important. Eyes closed or open — not at all important. All these are really "leaves and branches", trivialities.

Karma. Karma. You can redirect your karma by sitting more, by bowing more, by purifying the heart more and more.

Whether you believe in Buddhism or not, let me tell you this anyway. (And whether you believe or not what I'm going to say is again your karma.) Within X years, we will all successfully die. No one will fail. Nobody will fail! But that's not the end. The body may decay, but karma — karma — continues. And with appropriate conditions, it will be reborn — not "born" but formed in a different form. A different situation, a different name, but carrying the karma. Our practice can be defined as purifying the karma; shifting the direction of the karma.

One of the greatest contributions of Buddhism in the twentieth century has been to introduce this idea of karma to the West. And the second contribution is zazen practice.

•

On Pilgrimage

"Rinzai, while on a pilgrimage, arrived at Ryuko's temple."

A pilgrimage is a trip to visit holy places and sacred temples, but in a broader sense pilgrimage means from birth to death. And in an even broader sense, it means from the unknown beginning to the unknown ending. We say, "from beginningless beginning to endless end." Transmigration, transformation — we are all making a great pilgrimage without even stopping a day.

Here is a beautiful quotation on pilgrimage from "The Training of a Zen Buddhist Monk" by D.T. Suzuki: "Whence is birth, whither is death? He who knows this whence and whither is said to be a true Buddhist. But who is the one that knows birth and death? Who is the one that suffers birth and death? Who is the one that does not know whence birth is and whither death is? Who is the one who suddenly comes to the realization of this whence and whither? And who is the one that undergoes this torture? If you want to know who this one is, dive down into the depth of your being" — this is what zazen is — "where no intellection is possible. And when you do so, you know that there is a place neither birth nor death can touch."

This is very good! This short quotation is about pilgrimage in the narrow sense, the broader, and the broadest.

Instead of telling your friends that you're going on a retreat, say and know that you are going on a pilgrimage.

•

Renunciation

Why does someone become a monk or nun? This is very difficult to explain, but let's try.

Each one of you chose a certain profession, or a certain way to live. And some of you are quite contented with what you have chosen. But some of you may hear a gentle voice from some part of your heart saying, "You are doing well at what you have chosen but, so what?" That silent question, "So what?"

If you are one hundred percent contented with what you are doing, you don't have to become a monk. But from time to time, whether you are a doctor, socialworker, artist, businessperson, you may hear that voice. Something seems to be lacking and you want to fill up that hole. The reason why we meet at a zendo again and again is because, either consciously or unconsciously, we want to fill up that hole. So in a way, you are one-week monks and one-week nuns, or 45-minute monks, or weekend-workshop nuns.

Now, the difference between this "monk job" and other respected jobs or professions is that its clearly stated purpose is: Renunciation.

We don't usually use this term in other jobs and professions. This word has to do with "things", including psychological "things". Needing many things is the opposite of renouncing. Renunciation. Not needing things. When this is forgotten, or if it is not practiced, then there is not much difference between so-called ordained monks or nuns and ordinary people.

To be ordained a monk does not mean that, from that day on, one is a person of renunciation. You may shave your head as a visible act of renunciation, and year after year you may continue to shave your head, or wear your black robe. But this doesn't mean you have renounced aggression, arrogance, pride, greed, anger, or anything else. But a direction is set. A direction is set, at least.

So here we are, each with a different style of living, but the more we think about life, the more honest we are about our life. Sooner or later there is one way, only one way we will end up taking —

the path of a monk or a nun. I say, "Sooner or later." I do not mean necessarily within this lifetime. Sooner or later, many, many lives from now perhaps, we will eventually choose a direction. It will be quite different from all other directions, and it will be towards renunciation. That is the only way we can find peace of mind, and through it we can share that peace of mind with the people around us by our being, acts, and words.

All other "jobs" are almost the opposite of renunciation. You expect to gain, attain, obtain...along with the accompanying anxieties and suffering.

Perhaps this renunciation may seem naïve to you, idealistic. But those who have decided to become monks or nuns have gone through very delicate and complicated struggles to reach that point. And whatever the struggle, the key teaching and the key action is renunciation. They must always keep working in that direction.

Of course human beings are emotional beings. There is anger, and upset. But in the next moment they must tell themselves that they became monks and took the direction of renunciation. So, effort, effort, great effort. This requires not only this lifetime's effort, but life after life. When Harada Sogaku Roshi, Yasutani Roshi's teacher, was about to die at the age of ninety, someone asked, "Roshi, after your death, where will you go?" He said, "I will go to America, to be born in America, and to become a Buddhist monk in America."

The decision to become a monk or a nun doesn't come from just a few years of deep consideration. A few lives, more than a few, thinking it over, again and again. Then at last, when the karmic situation allows, you are ready to be ordained.

In this matter, monkhood, we have no choice. Sooner or later, we will all become monks and nuns. I'm positive that some of you right now in your heart are refusing to listen to what I'm saying. "Oh, not me," some of you may say. But allow me to speak, and I will allow you your resistance. There is no other choice, sooner or later.

The best way of life is to be ordained, and to renounce. Of course there is great difficulty in living this way in the twentieth century. We are not ancient Indians, or ancient Chinese, who were supported by their culture. Here in America right now Buddhism itself is so new. We talk very easily about "the spiritual life" but this life of renunciation in America, and even in Japan and in India these days, is not so easy. However, to shave the head is not so difficult, and to try to control our feelings is not so difficult.

Now, some of you think that to become a monk or a nun is to attain a new status. Monkhood is *not* a new status, not something special. To think it is, is not renunciation. "Now I'm something different" is not renunciation. I repeat that *everyone* knows what renunciation is, but monks and nuns are especially dedicated to this single point.

And when a certain degree of renunciation is reached, somehow Dharma helps. This is a most mysterious mechanism between renunciation and Dharma help. Of course we don't even expect Dharma aid. But when a certain degree of renunciation is actualized, the Dharma helps.

To wear the black robe, to shave the head, these represent the Dharma. Don't say, "But this is America." I'm talking about *Buddhist* monks and nuns. I'm not talking East or West. I'm sure many of you have seen Buddhist monks in a Theravadin country, with their shaved heads and orange robes, walking very quietly. Watching them is itself "ambrosial nectar" like today's rain. Somehow, seeing them, one's thirsty heart is refreshed. Something that is lacking is temporarily found.

To become a monk or a nun is a meritorious deed. You don't do it just to qualify to conduct funeral services. Sometimes you must do this, but monkhood in America is far more pure — by that I mean, more or less free of priestly responsibilities — than in Japan or some other places. You can renounce, and practice, and give positive vibrations to the people around you. Learning tranquility, peacefulness, clarity, lucidity, and contentment, and giving back these positive vibrations, and being thanked in some mysterious way — "What more need we seek?"

Daito Kokushi, Shuho Myocho Zenji, said, "Oh you monks, you are gathered in this deep mountain for the practice of renunciation, not for the food or the robes. And as long as you practice renunciation, the food comes all by itself; the robes come all by themselves."

Why they come, we don't fully understand but they do.

Those of you who are not going to be ordained immediately, please consider nevertheless that in zazen each sitting, each breath, is this renunciation. Of course I will not say such an unrealistic thing as, "Don't have any thoughts." But entertaining fewer thoughts in zazen is renunciation. Making less disturbance to sangha-living is renunciation. In that sense, all of us are doing the practice of renunciation even though only our two present candidates will have their heads shaved.

Do consider that all of us together are ordained.

•

Section IV

Teishos in the Rinzai Spirit

Introduction • 139
Open House • 141
What Is the Meaning? • 145
As-It-Is-ing • 151
He Walked and Walked • 155
No, They Don't • 163
On Meeting the Buddha • 169
Independence Day • 175
Can You "Do Nothing"? • 179
Leaving the Cage • 185

Introduction

Throughout this book I have been referring often to the Rinzai Roku, the sayings and doings of Master Rinzai. The purpose of this is to give you the flavor of what has become known as Rinzai Zen. Although I may use a koan from the various koan collections as a text for a teisho during sesshin, in the selections here I have more often used a quotation from the Rinzai Roku. In this way, reading, studying, and practicing, we appreciate the Zen patriarch called Master Rinzai, and we unite with all descendant Zen students and with future Dharma brothers and sisters.

Teishos appear to be talks given during sesshin, but there is a much larger meaning.

Each person's teisho is each person's manifested zazen. Everyone is giving teisho, mindfully or mindlessly, every moment. Even when we cannot attend sesshin, we are trying to develop our sensitivity, concentrate our attention, and broaden our compassion. And the results of these efforts can be seen by others.

Here is an example from monastery life, but you will understand the wider implications.

In the sutra-leader's book it says, "Strike bell three times." To strike ching, ching, ching, and to strike chiiing, chiinng, gchiing, are both "striking the bell." Nobody writes in the sutra book, "Please strike a serious, mindful, chiing, gchiing, gchiiing." Someone can write "Do it solemnly" but that can be interpreted in different ways. This is what each sutra-leader's teisho is: This day's manifested zazen, striking the bell.

So here are a few of my own teishos — my expressions, or my manifestations. Perhaps with the help of the preceding sections of this book, you will understand a little of what I am trying to say.

•

Open House

During the days when Dai Bosatsu Zendo was being built and its budget was all arranged, you may remember that we had all the upset of the oil embargo and inflation. I was becoming very involved in the problems of building and I couldn't seem to escape the madness of all those problems. I couldn't seem to do anything about them. I couldn't control anything that was happening in the world. I felt powerless, helpless, limited.

Here is an idea for you to remember for the future when you encounter something similar — that is, when you can't go forward, or backward, or stay in one place.

I thought it would be best for me to seclude myself for a week. I stayed at a cottage on the DBZ property. I did eat, and I did sleep. But I also did Open House. I opened my heart. I opened my being. I invited the Universal Energy, sun energy, moon energy, stars energy, animal energy, human energy, tree energy, rock energy, lake energy, to come into me as I chanted. I chanted the Bright Light Dharani:

On abo kya,
Bei rosha no,
Maka bo da ra,
Mani han, do ma jim, ba ra
Hara bari ta ya un.

I chanted this many, many, many, many, many times.

When you're confronted by some kind of problem and are feeling hopelessness or limitation, one of the things you can do is hold Open House. That is, open up your heart.

Don't think "I'm a small individual, my heart is not large enough, I'm not capable of doing such a thing." That's what I call the bumpkin vista. Seclude yourself and do Open House and invite — cordially invite — all Universal Energy to visit you. Amazingly enough, you will gradually feel that you are more than you think you are. You can do more than you think you can.

In return, you can radiate your own being. You don't have to speak. Your being speaks, and that silent speech is more eloquent than eloquent speech.

I learn these things from zazen. Master Hakuin said, "As for zazen in the Mahayana, we have no words to praise it fully." No matter how much we say about it, we never can fully praise it. You can define zazen many, many different ways but one way is "unification". That is, Open House. Open yourself. Open your being and, without fear, allow the Universal Energy to enter you.

Fear is a big problem. Some of us fear that some project we want to try will fail. Sometimes we feel guilty if we *don't* do some project. We don't want to feel guilty of being lazy but we don't want to fail. This is a big problem. Zen Buddhism offers a very clear answer for this.

You may not believe now what I'm going to say but what you see now, what you hear, what you smell, what you taste, what you sense, what you feel — these are not as tangible as you are convinced they are. These are temporary manifestations. You think they are real and that is where the mistake is. Let me speak from the realm of the *really* real. When the time comes, after you have done zazen with intense concentration, you will realize that what you can imagine in your own mind is not all there is. Listening to talks, reading books, and from the imaginings that grow from your own fear or your own wish, you may think you have formed a perfect picture of, for instance, "kensho". A hundred people will have a hundred expectations of kensho. "This is what it *ought* to be." Unfortunately and strangely enough, this fixed image is a great impediment to spiritual growth. What actually happens is not at all what you now imagine. What happens — and here I am talking about it and you will create more images, but this is human karma — what happens is the realization of shunyata.

What I feel now is that I exist: I feel pain; I feel joy; I feel sorrow. I can talk, listen, think, taste, and I can imagine. But what happens in a true realization is that all these are gone, gone, gone. And this is where our imagination cannot take us. We can imagine some things gone but we cannot imagine the earth is gone, the moon is gone, the universe is gone. And yet, something is able to recognize that all is gone. My own invented name for this something is "pure consciousness". This "pure consciousness" doesn't belong to me; it belongs to everyone. You ask, "Who tells, who knows, that everything is gone?" Just pure consciousness tells us. And in the next moment, all of a sudden, revitalization takes place. I am more me; it is more it.

When that revitalization takes place, whether it is strong or still weak, very clear or still not too clear, we do see that all the fears we had are completely unnecessary.

The Diamond Sutra says: "All composite things are like a dream, like a fantasy, like a bubble, like a dewdrop, like a flash of lightning." Things look as though they exist but they are ungraspable, ungrabbable. "So should you think of all this fleeting world." Intellectually, we cannot regard all things this way. Experientially, we have no choice but to do this.

And when this is done, the fear of failure, of becoming a failure, will be gone. The desire for this project or that project to succeed will also be gone. This doesn't mean we become lazy. Rather, we now can appreciate, moment after moment, truly appreciate, the breath, air, water, our temporary existence, temporary friendship, temporary project, temporary every thing. That's what, after all, our practice is for. Unless we reach that vista, that viewing point, real peace of mind will never come. We will always be discontented.

Now here is a play on words, but important. Discontented. Content, as in "contentment". Content, as in "what is inside a container". Discontented — having no contents. Referring again to Open House, consider your own being; consider this your own house. This is a container — flesh, blood, apple, couscous, brain, feeling, thinking. Many, many contents, yet we say we are *dis*-contented! We have a container and more than enough contents, including Buddha Nature, and we still say we are discontented!

Some people say, "Well, this content is not what I want. If the content is replaced, I will be contented." Never. Even with change after change after change, you will never be contented. Contentment is right now! As you *are*!

•

What Is the Meaning?

Text: Hekigan Roku (The Blue Cliff Collection), Case 73: Baso and the Hundred Negations

> A monk said to Baso, "Independent of the four propositions and transcending the hundred negations, tell me the meaning of Bodhidharma's coming from the West."
>
> Baso said, "Today I am tired and cannot tell you. Ask Chizo about it."
>
> The monk asked Chizo, who said, "Why don't you ask the Master?" The monk replied, "He told me to ask you." Chizo said, "Today I have a headache and cannot tell you about it. Ask brother Ekai."
>
> The monk asked Ekai, who said, "At this point, I do not understand."
>
> The monk told this to Baso, who said, "Chizo's head is white, Ekai's head is black."

This text is one of the two favorites of Hakuun Shitsu Yasutani Ryoko Zenji. It seems to me he liked this one and Joshu's Mu the most of all the koans. It is with gratitude to Yasutani Roshi that I present this now.

The key phrase for today's teisho is "Tell me the meaning of Bodhidharma's coming from the West?"

Why did Bodhidharma come from India to China? If we try to understand this koan literally, and if we ask why the venerable historical figure, Bodhidharma, took a journey from India to China, and if we expect an answer to begin, "Because...", then we will not get anywhere.

We're not asking why? or, how come? in the ordinary sense. We're not talking about a Chinese story. We're not talking about the history of Zen Buddhism. We're pointing to each fact as an event, using "event" in the same sense as it is used in the

Bodhisattva's Vow. "In any event, in any moment, and in any place...." Or better, in *each* event, in *each* moment, and in *each* place, Buddha Nature is being revealed, or Bodhidharma is coming from the West. And if you make a link between this strange question, "Why did Bodhidharma come from the West?" and the phrases, *this* event, *this* moment, *this* place — if you can make this link, then this koan is extremely easy to understand.

Yasutani Roshi often said at the beginning of this koan, "Listen *very* carefully." He used the expression "white-paper attitude." And, "By the end of my talk, all of you can be enlightened." He said this for the first time in America in the days when people were talking kensho, kensho, kensho, enlightenment, enlightenment. And people really paid attention, really listened, but...nobody was enlightened. But that too is nothing but the coming of Bodhidharma from India to China.

We all tend to interpret things literally. We live in an existential world.

For instance, we say in the Dedication, "Let us unite with...." We think it means this: Normally, we are separate individuals but at this moment let us make the effort to unite with.... But this is the limitation of language. What we really mean is: Let us realize that from the beginningless beginning we have been united and cannot be separated. Realize this fact. There will never be a separation between "we" or "I" and Endless Dimension Universal Life.

To keep our sentences short and simple we say, This Matter. If we say, "The coming of Bodhidharma from West to East," or "What is the sound of one hand clapping?" or "What is your original true nature before your great-grandparents were born?" or "Mu," then there is a confused and exotic atmosphere. But all these can be expressed as This Matter.

This Matter must not be seen as human emotion. We say that birth is happy, death is sad, and this is true from an ordinary point of view. But because of this emotional aspect we miss the point. Birth is This Matter, death is This Matter, meeting each other is This Matter, fighting is This Matter, good health is This Matter, illness is This Matter. But we are human beings and we have preferences. I like some of these matters but not others. Perfectly understandable. Zen Buddhism does not deny it. But Zen Buddhism makes this point: Preference or attachment is an impediment to seeing This Matter. We do zazen in order to transcend this sticky human attachment. And by transcending these sticky attachments we see event as event, each thing as each thing, not otherwise than the condensed manifestation of universal energy.

So in a teisho the only thing we stress repeatedly is "See This Matter!" Everybody is already seeing, hearing, tasting This Matter at this very moment but, because of our strange mental mechanism, we search for it somewhere outside.

Once This Matter is seen, of course sadness is sadness and joy is joy, but what I call the vista, the viewpoint, changes. The normal vista is to have preferences, but the transcendental vista is to see a thing as a thing, without judgments of good or bad, or liking or disliking. At the moment of seeing This Matter, each of us realizes that we cannot be *otherwise* than Buddha Nature. It's not that we have become Buddha but that we realize we cannot be other than Buddha Nature.

Looking at things this way, each event of a morning in the zendo is This Matter — a leg hurting, sleepiness, less oxygen in a crowded room, a neighbor restless, and so on. This Matter! The reason we cannot understand these events as This Matter is that we think each event can be improved. "If I shift my leg, it won't hurt. If I could get more sleep, I wouldn't be so sleepy. If only they'd open a window, I could breathe." The idea that things can be improved comes from our greed. Our greed is none other than our attachment. We are humans. I'm not denying human desire, but I'm pointing out that because of desire we suffer. Or, because of desire and attachment we cannot see this matter as This Matter.

This is the story, so "listen carefully."

A monk said to Baso, "Independent of the four propositions and transcending the hundred negations..." — apart from all these complicated theologies and philosophies, tell me about This Matter *directly*.

Baso said, "Today I am tired and cannot tell you."

Wonderful? "Today I am tired and cannot tell you." This is This Matter. Do not interpret it this way: "What's the matter with Baso, the great Zen master? How come he's so exhausted?"

"Today I am tired and cannot tell you. Ask Chizo about it."

The monk did not realize what was really being said, so he went to Chizo's place. This is also This Matter! He asked the same question.

Chizo said, "Why don't you ask the Master?"

This too is This Matter!

The monk replied, "He told me to ask you."

Chizo said, "Today I have a headache and cannot tell you about it." And maybe he did have a great headache. But still this monk evidently did not see This Matter. So Chizo kindly suggested, "Ask brother Ekai" (Hyakujo Ekai Zenji).

The monk came to Hyakujo's place and asked the real meaning of This Matter. "Master Baso was tired today, and Chizo has a headache, and they told me to ask you."

Hyakujo said, "I simply don't know."

Now, it's rather important for us to think about this "I don't know." We think we can know everything or we deserve to know everything or we are capable of knowing everything. But the truth is, we don't know even very simple facts. On this morning, why are there just this many people here in the zendo? Why not one more? If that one more had a headache, why did he have it? We don't know. We must not think we know things. Of course, we know how to count from one to ten. We know what is up and what's down. We know to express condolences at a funeral, and congratulations at a wedding. But we cannot know more than that. I used to ask, Why? why? why? Now my favorite expression is, "For some reason...." For some reason, a certain number of us are gathered here this morning.

We are deceived by language. If we say, This is it! we may mean the end of the world. If we say, THIS! IS! IT! we are manifesting the Zen tradition. Someone will say, "That flower is white." More precisely, "That white tulip is a white tulip." Even more precise would be, "That tulip is tulip-ing." Irritation is irritation-ing. Pain is pain-ing. Thus we chant, "When I, a student of Dharma, look at the real form of the universe, all is the never-failing manifestation of the mysterious truth..." — it's not at all mysterious — ...truth of This Matter. In each event, in each moment, and in each place, none can be other than the marvelous revelation of its glorious light.

So Ekai said, "At this point, I do not understand."

The travelling monk, even though he had received such wonderful teishos from three different teachers, still thought, "What's the matter with this monastery? The head roshi is exhausted, the second has a headache, the third doesn't understand." And not knowing that even *confusion* is This Matter, he returned to Baso who said, "Chizo's head is white; Ekai's head is black."

> "In Spring, hundreds of flowers.
> In Summer, refreshing breeze.
> In Autumn, harvest moon.
> In Winter, snowflakes accompany you.
> If useless things do not hang in your mind, every season is the best season."

Useless things, attachments, and preferences. Drop them! Then every year is the best year. Every day is the best day. Every moment is the highest moment!

This is not theory but truth. Whether we can accept it or not is a matter of our maturity, how mature, how lucid our zazen is.

Therefore, sit more, endure pain to do it, and attend sesshin.

•

As-It-Is-ing

Text: Hekigan Roku (Blue Cliff Collection), Case 51: Seppo's What Is This?

> When Seppo was living in his hermitage, two monks came to pay their respects. As Seppo saw them coming, he pushed open the gate and, presenting himself before them, said, "What is this?"
> The monks also said, "What is this?"
> Seppo lowered his head and returned to his hut.
> Later, the monks came to Ganto who said, "Where have you come from?" The monks answered, "We have come from south of the Nanrei Mountains."
> Ganto said, "Have you been to see my Dharma brother Seppo?"
> The monks said, "Yes."
> Ganto asked, "What did he say to you?" The monks related the story.
> Ganto said, "Alas, I regret that I did not tell him the last word when I was with him. If I had done so, no one in the whole world could have pretended to outdo him."
> At the end of the summer training session, the monks repeated the story and asked Ganto for his instruction.
> Ganto said, "Why didn't you ask earlier?" The monks replied, "We have had a hard time struggling with this."
> Ganto said, "Seppo came to life in the same way I did, but he does not die in the same way I do. If you want to know the last word, I will tell you. Just This, This!"

Today's text was Soen Roshi's favorite.

Let me say a few words about Zen koans or Zen dialogue. We can't help but think that a koan is something exotic or mysterious and that it might have some kind of magic power. But "koan" really means the place and the time and the event where truth reveals itself. Where reality is revealed. Of course we know by now that there is no place or event or time when the truth is not revealed. When you do zazen with a flood of thoughts, *that* event is the truth, floodingly revealed. That is an everyday-life koan.

When Seppo saw the travelling monks coming, he presented himself before them and said, "What is this?"

(We know from Bassui Tokusho Zenji's writing that instead of repeating Mu, Mu, Mu, Seppo used the practice of What is this? What is this?)

Seppo lived in a period of persecution when many monks hid themselves. Seppo was living in a small cottage, doing zazen, and he didn't see other human beings very often. So he went out to greet the monks. But instead of asking, "What's going on in the capital? What's the attitude of the government?" he simply presented, "What is this?" What is *This*? Ganto later answered the question, "After all, what is this?" He said, "Just This!"

Western science has had a fantastic development by asking, what is this? If there's an object, a phenomenon, then some answer can be given. But without such an object, what can the answer be? This is one of the most important koans. Instead of putting their palms together in gratitude, the monks imitated Seppo and said, "What is this?"

Must we stop asking questions? No more progress? Must we accept this as this? There is a fear in our hearts or in our minds. We feel we must make some kind of progress.

But no matter how much progress we make, just this!

There is a wonderful expression: As-it-isness. Or, suchness. As-it-is-ing is even better. Why? It's more alive, more direct. As-it-is-ing. Such-ing. "Tulip-ing!" This is the advantage of a foreigner; we can be creative with the language. We don't depend on dead idioms. As-it-is-ing. This is not negative. It is eternal pro-gress-ing, endlessly revealing at this very moment.

We modern people are very analytical. But no matter how we analyze "What is this?" there is no answer. This is it! Oriental people are trained to accept their karma instead of trying to erase it. By openly accepting what we are, the gate opens even more. But this is so delicate....

The point is, no matter where we are from, as human beings we want to be contented, happier. We say "just this" is too simple. We must have something more profound. We desire, and analyze, and search, search, search. Thus we suffer frustration, confusion, and exhaustion too. We're afraid that if we accept "just this" we'll be considered stupid. But where is the real stupidity? If I may say, it's in the waste of time and energy in desire and analysis and the added confusion. What is this? Just this-ing. Is-ing.

By now you understand what I want to convey. Still, the habits of many years are not easily changed. Zen Buddhism is trying to teach us to stop resisting this as this. It can only be done with sufficient zazen energy. When we accumulate zazen energy, without fear, without suspicion, this reveals as This! And we can simply put our palms together. At that moment, we are contented. Until that moment comes, contentment is merely an "imaginary flower in the air."

What Yasutani Roshi and Soen Roshi taught us, I'm still digesting and translating into Western thinking. With their teaching, and zazen practice, we will learn "What is this?" Just This!

•

He Walked and Walked

Text: Rinzai Roku, Record of Pilgrimages I and XXII (biography)

At Obaku's monastery the head monk had the Dharma eye. That means he was discerning — "discern" is an excellent English word. He was impressed by what he saw of Rinzai. He said to Obaku, "Although he is a youngster, he is different from the other monks." Some people, while physically quite old, are immature. Others are physically young but mentally matured, and we see many examples around here. Nobody knows how old Rinzai was because his birth-year is unknown but we assume he was between twenty-five and thirty, which is considered young in these circumstances. "He is different from the others," the head monk said to Obaku.

One day, the head monk asked Rinzai, "How long have you been here?"

Rinzai replied, "Three years."

This is not totally correct. But at the same time, it is not totally incorrect either. This is where we see the other aspect of thinking. If you don't understand it right now, think about it.

Rinzai, in modern terminology, had received his Bachelor's degree and, from graduate school, his Master's degree and then his PhD, specializing in Buddhist studies. But one day, with a great sigh, he said to himself, "This is not the way to salvation." So he changed clothes from his jeans to a black robe, came to a Zen monastery, and sat down!

Evidently Rinzai had been at Obaku's monastery for three years, working, studying, doing zazen, bowing.

"Have you ever asked for instruction?"

"No."

Even if this is what I call Chinese exaggeration, it's still quite a long time. No instruction, no orientation, no question-and-answer periods — just being there.

This is one important part of Zen tradition: saturation. Learning to see how things are done and following along, your body becomes saturated with Zen ways. Three years in the library and you can learn many things but they are easily forgotten. Let your body learn and you never forget. In ancient, and in modern, monastic tradition, let the body be saturated. Then you learn when the *han* is struck too loudly, or the gong. Someone shouts at you. "Why? I have to think." And in a few days, "Oh, I see." Then you never forget. No teaching, no instruction, just shouting: "No good!" No good what? You figure it out, and you remember. You don't remember when you are instructed sweetly.

So three years were not wasted time for Rinzai. I'm sure no one taught him the full-lotus sitting position. Nobody taught him how to straighten his spine, how to place his hands. No one taught him how to strike the *mokugyo* or how to strike the gong. Nobody teaches, but we learn by listening and participating. This is called saturation. When we struggle, we never forget.

And, who knows? It may be that some Dharma student, listening to the han being struck just right — with concern, concern — or walking in kinhin at just the right pace, or hearing the gong sound exactly right, will be able to open his or her Dharma eye. This "rightness" we can only learn by saturation. Quiet dynamism. Dynamic quietness.

GOONNGG! is not dynamism. That's called loudness.

I'm sure no one insisted that Rinzai hold his hands with the right one on top and the left one below, or vice-versa. At the end of our trip to China in 1981, we sat with Chinese monks at a zendo, and after zazen there was actually a question-and-answer period. We had noticed that some of the monks did the hand mudra with the left hand on top, and some with the right. Someone said, "I have been told that the left is below and the right is above." One monk was very impressive. His impressive words were, "It doesn't matter."

And he is right! It *doesn't* matter. When Shakyamuni Buddha was enlightened under the Bo Tree, no one recorded whether his left hand was on top of his right hand or not. The fact is, he gained great insight.

"Have you ever asked for instruction?"

"I don't know what to ask," said Rinzai.

Most likely, the monk Rinzai knew all the "trivial" things by watching and observing and practicing. He knew how to chant, how to sit, how to loosen his diaphragm so that his breath went all the way down all the time, and his head was cool and lucid all the time. Therefore, with a slight arrogance that he was probably not aware of, he said, "I don't know what to ask."

"Why don't you go ask Obaku Kiun Zenji what the cardinal principle of the Buddhadharma is?"

We are deceived by this expression, Buddhadharma. We think it's something to do with Buddhism. We think there is no Buddhadharma in Christianity. Buddhism is this, and Judaism is this, and Christianity is divided into many pieces — that's the way we think. And this is not totally incorrect, but we have to be very, very careful. We have this habit of categorizing. There is Buddhadharma in all these traditions.

Someone came to me and said, "At last I understand the expression 'when I sit, the entire universe sits'. When I walk, the entire universe walks. But the moment I start to think about it, it is difficult...." She was struggling to express herself.

When one sits, the entire universe sits. When one is confused, the entire universe is confused. This is not a matter of intellectual comprehension. If we try to comprehend it intellectually, this is the question we end up with: "If she sits, the universe sits, and if I move, the universe moves — how can one universe move and sit simultaneously?" This is the limitation of the intellect. But the truth is, when she sits, the entire universe sits. At the same time, when I move, the entire universe moves. When he laughs, certainly the entire universe laughs, and when someone cries, the entire universe cries.

The entire universe is so busy! How can all this be possible? How can one entire universe meet all these requirements? This is the limitation of our intellectual comprehension. The "cardinal principle of Buddhadharma" is to understand that when one sits, the entire universe sits. When one cries, the entire universe cries.

So Rinzai, with plain and direct behavior, went to Obaku Kiun Zenji, bowed low, and asked, "What is the cardinal principle of Buddhadharma?" Before he had finished speaking, Obaku struck him!

By now you know that this hitting — This! Is! It! — is one way to express, perhaps inadequately, the "cardinal principle of Buddhadharma." Suchness! Thisness! As-it-isness! Obaku does *not* hit Rinzai to express, "Don't ask stupid questions!"

But Rinzai did not understand and came back to the waiting head monk.

"How did your question go?" asked the head monk. Rinzai replied, "Before I had finished speaking, Master Obaku struck me. I don't understand."

This is *so* good! This is being plain and direct in his behavior.

"Then go and ask him again!"

This sentence and this way of saying it — instead of, "Oh I'm sorry to hear that, he must be in a bad mood, perhaps you should try tomorrow" — this Zen activity, this spontaneous decisiveness with forceful dynamism — this is called *ki*. Zen ki. We must learn this. Without ki, Zen is not vital.

"Then go and ask him again!"

So Rinzai went back and once more he asked, "Master, what is the cardinal principle of...?"

THIS!

Three times. Or maybe it was five times, or one hundred times. How many of us are brave enough for this? But this is *exactly* what Mu-practice should be. "Mu." THIS! "Mu." THIS!

All this is preparation.

Rinzai came back to the head monk. "I asked the question three times (or thirty) and I was hit each time. I regret that some obstruction caused by my own karma prevents me from grasping his profound meaning. I'm going away for a while."

Now here's another example of ki. The head monk said to

Rinzai, "All right. But if you're going away, you should take leave of the Master."

Before Rinzai took his leave, the head monk went to Obaku and said, "The young man who has been questioning you is a man of Dharma. When he comes to take his leave, please handle him expediently. In the future, with training, he is sure to become a great tree that will provide cool shade for the people of the world."

Now we have the so-called Rinzai School and, in one way or another, we are receiving his "cool shade" in these rather confused days.

Rinzai is taking his leave of Obaku. Because of his own karma, he thinks, he cannot understand Obaku's teaching. And the head monk has asked Obaku to "handle the young monk expediently."

So Obaku said, "You must not go anywhere else but to Daigu's monastery. He's sure to explain things for you."

It is not a matter of explaining. Nobody can *explain*. What he meant was, he is sure to open your eyes.

So with plain and direct spirit, Rinzai accepted Obaku's suggestion and walked, walked, walked, walked, and at last arrived at Daigu's temple. This long walking is the same as participating in many, many sesshins, in many, many kesseis, or spending many years learning to make a bowl of tea.

Daigu said, "Where have you come from?"

As an unenlightened monk, remember, Rinzai said, "I have come from Mount Obaku."

"What did Obaku have to say?" Or in other words, What is my Dharma brother's teaching style nowadays?

Monk Rinzai said, "Three times I asked him what the cardinal principle of Buddhadharma was and three times he hit me. I don't know whether I was at fault or not."

He thought he was at fault, even if unknowingly, and that's why he was hit. He was still thinking it had something to do with right or wrong, fault or no fault. That's the level he was thinking at.

Daigu said, "My Dharma brother Obaku is such a grandmother. He utterly exhausts himself with your troubles."

Utterly exhausting himself is a kind of transmission, giving his nen energy, zazen energy, Dharma energy, to his dear students.

Daigu doesn't hit Rinzai but he is saying, "Obaku is utterly exhausting himself for you and you are asking whether you're at fault or not? What's the matter with you?"

At these words, we are told, Rinzai attained great enlightenment.

Words, words.... With words we are hurt; with words we are made happy; with words we are disturbed; with words we are confused; with words we clarify. What to say, how to say it, when to say it — in Zen practice this is *so* important. Words are influential — powerful, powerful. Just think of Joshu's Mu!

At these words, Rinzai attained great insight. He understood This Matter. Until this time he had been deceived by such expressions as "the cardinal principle of Buddhadharma". Now he understood.

Then Rinzai said, "Ah, there's not so much to Obaku's Buddhadharma."

He meant, there's nothing special about these expressions. Nothing special.

We want to be special. We want to seek something special. We want to regard something as special. But in truth, even "special" is after all nothing special. Remember, "When tired, rest; when hungry, eat; when sleepy, sleep." Nothing special. "Fools laugh at me, but the wise understand."

So there's really nothing special about Buddhadharma.

Now here comes the normal question. If it's nothing special, how come we have to do sesshin? How come we have to endure the mental and physical and psychological pain? The answer to this is, we must *realize* that nothing is special. Things are as they are. This is the natural koan, probably, for most people these days. "*Nyo ze.*" Thusness. As-it-isness. We want to know more than as-it-isness. We want to analyze. We want to categorize. We want to specialize.

Daigu grabbed hold of Rinzai, with Zen ki of course, and said, "You bed-wetting little devil!" (It is better to be gentle *most* of the time, but once in ten years, maybe....) "You just finished asking whether you are at fault or not. Now you say there isn't so much to Obaku's Buddhadharma. What did you just see?! Speak!"

Of course Rinzai couldn't speak of what he had just understood, and he didn't need to speak. So he jabbed Daigu in the side, three times. Even once is okay. It doesn't have to be the side; the front is okay. Or you can just put palms together and bow. *With* understanding, whatever you do is okay. Without understanding, whatever you do or say is *not* okay. So don't be deceived about phrases such as "three times in the side".

So Rinzai came back to Obaku who said, "What a fellow, coming and going, coming and going. When will it end?"

Now this is a very interesting question. When will it end? Not just Rinzai's coming and going but our life, our Zen practice, when will it end? When did it start? This is a koan for all of us to think about.

Rinzai told his teacher about his first kensho experience, at Daigu's monastery. Obaku was so happy!

I have read this part of the Rinzai Roku so many times, in Chinese and in English, and each time I learn something new.

•

No, They Don't

Text: Rinzai Roku, Critical Examinations XII

> One day, the Councillor Wang visited Master Rinzai. When he met the Master in front of the monks' hall he asked, "Do the monks of this monastery chant sutras?"
> "No, they don't chant sutras," said Rinzai.
> "Then do they study Zen?" asked the Councillor. "No, they don't study Zen," answered Master Rinzai.
> "If they neither chant sutras nor study Zen, what in the world are they doing?" asked the Councillor.
> "All I do is help them become buddhas and patriarchs," said the Master.
> The Councillor said, "Though gold dust is precious, when it gets into the eyes, it clouds the vision."
> "I always used to think you were just a common fellow. But now I know that you are not," said Master Rinzai.

"One day...." Again, I repeat this business of "one day". It is not, one of these many days, or one particular day it so happened.... That's bumpkin vista. *One* day. *One.* Obaku Kiun Zenji said, "One Mind" — he didn't mean, out of perhaps five minds this was one of them. The same is true of this One Day — not one of maybe five. This one day, nothing else. So it is with today's story. It is not taking place in Sung Dynasty China.

The Councillor Wang was a student of Issan Reiyu Zenji who, with his disciple Kyosan, founded the Zen School called the Igyo Shu. Evidently this Councillor Wang was not an ordinary man but had at least entered the lake of shunyata. He came to see Rinzai Gigen Zenji. That in itself is a beautiful picture, even a poem. And then I assume they had a cup of tea. And then both giants decided to take a walk and they walked all the way to the front of our zendo.

The Councillor Wang asked Master Rinzai, "Do the monks chant sutras?"

Master Rinzai said, "No, they don't chant sutras."

This kind of dialogue is so deep that it's easily misinterpreted. As long as it's a Buddhist monastery, all kinds of sutras are chanted — Maka Hannya Haramita Shin Gyo, Namu Samanda, Enmei Jukku Kannon Gyo, Namu Kara Tan No, Myoho Renge Kyo, and so on. But these two people are not talking on that level. They're talking on the teisho level, or shunyata level, or profound-vista level. So Master Rinzai said, "No, they don't," implying that there is a broader meaning to sutra-chanting. Like, "No heaven, no earth, just snow falling." That kind of sutra is always being chanted, whether in a Christian monastery, or Buddhist monastery, or Atheistic monastery if there is such — from morning to morning, constant sutra-chanting. And of course Councillor Wang understood, and Rinzai understood the Councillor's intention.

He asked a second question: "Do they study Zen?" Study Ch'an? Study Dhyana? Or you might ask, Do they practice zazen on the cushion? It is only in the narrowest sense that we would say yes, they practice zazen. In the broadest sense, no, they don't study Zen. There is no "Zen" as such to study!

Again, this is where language makes things so difficult. Here comes an explanation, but the moment something is explained, there is material for excuses. With this risk, let me try.

Whether standing or sitting, whether concentrating or dozing, whether confused or lucid, whether dead or alive, whether it is sesshin or non-sesshin time, there is not a thing, from the profound-vista viewpoint, that is not Zen. So Master Rinzai said, "No, they don't study Zen." In fact, they cannot! From the shunyata viewpoint, *there is no Zen to study.*

Whether you shout Mu! or don't, it doesn't matter. But this is where the excuses start. If it doesn't matter, we might as well take the easy way. Now, it "doesn't matter" from the shunyata viewpoint, but it *does* matter from the practice viewpoint. From the practice viewpoint, don't doze! Shout! Concentrate! "Does matter, doesn't matter" — you see how language mixes us up.

I use the example of ocean and wave. They are the same thing in one sense, and yet different, and yet the same. They are inseparable. Therefore we sometimes speak of this fundamental reality, this shunyata matter, and at the same time, we speak of this phenomenological reality. This is where there are two, yet one, yet two. There is mixup and confusion, and the finding of good excuses. That's why we often say, "Stop talking and just sit." This is really the limitation of language; at this point we have to stop talking. And at *this* point where language ends, Zen practice begins.

So Master Rinzai said, "No, they don't study Zen."

Similar questions can be asked.

Do they memorize sutras? No, they don't memorize sutras.

Do they clean? No. The monastery is fundamentally pure. But existentially dusty. We're used to hearing existential instructions. Today is cleaning day. Do the basement shoe-room. Do the second-floor bathroom. That's clear, and they need to be done. But a teisho is guiding us into new dimensions. "No, they don't clean." Why? Because we're fundamentally pure. So it sounds good: we don't have to do anything. We don't have to study, we don't have to clean.

But in order to come to that understanding, that realization, we must work hard, hard, hard! Pushing. Being pushed! Then, aaahh! We are reborn, so to speak, and this rebirth while we are still alive is called, in the Rinzai tradition, kensho.

This is the most significant way to live, the most meaningful way to live. Who am I? What is this Mu? All can be answered from shunyata. It is that which creates us. Everything comes from there. We have to go back there. Not "there" but here! That's why we sit, sit, sit, sit.

While you are doing Mu, repeating Mu is fine. But at the same time, we have to question, *What* is Mu? What, why, how? Why did the monk ask, "Does a dog have Buddha Nature?" *Why* did Joshu say, "Mu"? All kinds of questions, from many different angles, and we shout, shout, repeat, repeat, repeat. And it's not this one student of Dharma who, as we think, is a "separated individuality" doing Mu. Rather, the *entire* universe, from above heaven to below the earth, from the unbounded above to the boundless below — sometimes "universe" alone is a dead word — the *entire* universe — is doing Mu, is Mu-ing. Universal-concentration Mu, sitting after sitting, kinhin after kinhin, sesshin after sesshin....

It is very difficult to do this work alone so we gather together. Yasutani Roshi said something like this: "A piece of green wood is not combustible by itself. But together with well-dried wood in the fire, it combusts!" There are plenty of well-dried pieces of wood in this sesshin, so if someone is attending for the first time and if that someone cannot combust alone, then together...!!

"If they neither chant sutras nor study Zen, then what in the world are they doing?" asked the Councillor.

Master Rinzai replied, "All I do is help them become buddhas and patriarchs."

All I do is help them realize this unshakable, unchangeable shunyata reality. I make them testify to that. I make them go there and look from there. Then all beings are Buddha. Otherwise, all beings are bumpkins. Reciting Hakuin's "All beings are fundamentally Buddha" is better than nothing. But Master Hakuin didn't just recite it, he spoke from his shunyata experience. Even a dead raccoon, not to speak of good brothers and sisters in the Dharma, is a buddha or a patriarch. So Master Rinzai is saying: "All I wish, all I pray, encourage, direct, is toward one goal."

That's what we're doing here too.

"I always used to think you were just a common fellow, but now I know you are my friend."

Friend, not just knowing each other, but knowing each other in shunyata. I know shunyata, he knows shunyata, in shunyata we are in common. That's a real friend even though there are sometimes personality differences. Sometimes many differences occur but so long as we are in common in shunyata, then we are friends. No matter how intimate two people may be, if they don't share shunyata, they just have temporary togetherness. They don't understand the profundity of life.

So, brothers and sisters, please do your best, *your* best, *your!* best. Your today's BEST!

·

On Meeting the Buddha

Text: Rinzai Roku, Discourses XVIII

> Followers of the Way, he who is a renouncer of home must needs study the Way. Take me, for example. In bygone days, I devoted myself to the Vinaya and also delved into the sutras and shastras. Later, when I realized that they were merely medicines for salvation and displays of doctrines in written words, I once and for all threw them away and, searching for the Way, I practiced zazen. Still later, I met great teachers. Then it was, with my Dharma eye becoming clear, that I could discern all the old teachers under heaven and tell the false ones from the true. It is not that I understood from the moment I was born of my mother but that, after exhaustive investigation and grinding discipline, in an instant I knew my True Self.
>
> Followers of the Way, if you want insight into Dharma as it is, just don't be taken in by the deluded views of others. Whatever you encounter, either within or without, slay it at once. On meeting the Buddha, slay the Buddha. On meeting a patriarch, slay the patriarch. On meeting an arhat, slay the arhat. On meeting your parents, slay your parents. On meeting your kinsman, slay your kinsman, and you attain emancipation. By not clinging to things, you freely pass through.

The text today is only one part of a section of Rinzai's discourse called "True Insight". Someone has said that the best English translation for kensho is not "enlightenment" but "insight". True insight.

Rinzai is speaking to the monks at his temple by the Koda River in Chinshu Province. To this marvelously karmically formed assembly — like us here — he was saying, "Followers of the Way, he who is a renouncer of home must needs study the Way." I assume the participants in those days were all monks who were "renouncers of home". But for this sesshin in the midst of twentieth century civilization, we too have renounced family and work for seven days and must study the Way. "Must" is a strong word but yet not strong enough.

Rinzai says, "Take me for example. In bygone days I devoted myself to the Vinaya." Devoted! Vinaya means the study of the precepts. In some traditions of Buddhism there are twenty or 250, or 500 precepts to follow. Do, don't do, don't do, do. He devoted himself to commandments, and delved into and searched into the sutras, especially Kegon, the highest philosophical formulation of the Buddhist tradition. He studied the shastras, commentaries on the sutras, and many other things. In other words, he studied, studied, studied.

"Later, when I realized that they were merely medicines for salvation and displays of doctrines in written words, I once and for all threw them away and, searching for the Way, I practiced zazen."

A similar story can be found about Tokusan Senkan Zenji. At the time, he was a scholar of the Diamond Sutra. He heard that a new school called Zen had just come to China. He carried about with him all the sutras and shastras in order to defeat Zen people in argument. One time, he stopped at a sort of coffee-and-pastry shop run by an elderly enlightened woman.

She said to Tokusan, "Where are you from?"

"I'm from the north. May I have a cup of tea and a piece of cake, please?"

She said, "Of course, if you can answer my question. First, who are you?"

"I am Tokusan, king of the Diamond Sutra."

"I have a question regarding the Diamond Sutra."

"Yes, what is it?"

"In Chapter 18 it says, 'Past mind is ungraspable, present mind is ungraspable, and future mind is also ungraspable.' With which mind do you grasp a cup of tea and a piece of cake?"

Tokusan could not answer this question. He humbly said, "There must be someone who taught you something profound."

The wise lady suggested he go to Ryutan's temple.

He went, and he talked to Ryutan for hours and hours. At night the electricity went off, the way it did here last night, and it was dark. Internal as well as external dark. For Tokusan, who had lost his confidence, it was *utter* darkness. And then — we know this now — it was the readiness of time. Ryutan sent Tokusan off to bed and the moment he handed Tokusan a lighted lantern, Ryutan blew it out! Again darkness, and it was this *darkness* that led Tokusan into shunyata.

The following day in front of Ryutan's temple, Tokusan burned all his books, notes, tapes, video tapes, transcripts....

"Later," says Rinzai, "when I realized that they were merely medicines for salvation and displays of doctrines in written words, I once and for all threw them away. Searching for the Way, I began the practice of zazen."

Nowadays, we start to practice zazen and we also read many, many books. In a way, it's a good thing. During sesshin, it's perhaps good to read *good* books, such as the Rinzai Roku, or Denshin Hoyo, or Huang Po's Transmission of Mind, or Dogen's Shobogenzo. Read with erect spine, and line by line — don't skim — and even read *between* lines, and one page at a time.

In Rinzai's case he studied and studied and read and read, and threw them all away. Finally he began zazen.

"Still later, I met great teachers," and we know that one of them was Huang Po, Obaku Kiun Zenji. Another was Daigu.

"Then it was, with my Dharma eye becoming clear, that I could discern all the teachers under heaven and tell the false ones from the true." If you have the clear Dharma eye, you can discern. True insight; that's all that's necessary.

True insight is the common ground.

For many summers I went to Naropa Institute for its Buddhist-Christian Conference. It was so clear that if Christian representatives talked on Christian theology and Buddhist representatives talked on Buddhist philosophy, this theology and philosophy never linked. But if both parties talked on such things as St. Benedict, the founder of the Benedictine Order in Catholic tradition and who, according to the stories of his life, obviously had true insight, and if we also talked about Rinzai's true insight, then there was common ground between Buddhism and Christianity. We *really* found common ground when talking about the true insight of Meister Eckhart.

"It is not that I understood from the moment I was born, but that after exhaustive investigation, and grinding discipline, in an instant, I knew my True Self." In other words, I studied, I did zazen, I met teachers — I didn't understand immediately from the moment I was born. *Exhaustive* investigation. *Grinding* discipline.

And the readiness of time. And then in one instant, I knew my True Self.

"Followers of the Way, if you want insight into Dharma as it is, just don't be taken in by the deluded views of others. Whatever you encounter, either within or without...."

Within, we have millions of feelings and thoughts; without, externally, millions of other distractions. So that's why we say in sesshin, "Don't look around," and we can minimize things to slay.

"...slay it at once!" Slay, slay! When you shout Mu, that's slaying. Thoughts: "Did I do it well?" Slay! Mu! until completely exhausted and no judgmental thoughts come. That's what "slay" means. "I would like to reserve my energy for the next shouting. I would like to do it when my condition is good. I would like to do it on the last day most dramatically." All kinds of I-would-like-to, slay! That's what slay! means.

Rinzai didn't say that on meeting the Buddha you should pay homage to the Buddha. He said, "Slay the Buddha." On meeting your parents, slay your parents. That is the best present for them. Not literally of course. But this is what we're doing here. Slay me, slay the "deluded views of others," slay thoughts, desires, wishes, hopes. This is a key point of Rinzai's teaching. How do we do it? Mu! Muuuuuu. "...and you attain your emancipation." You "get it".

That's shunyata. Translations of "emptiness" or "void" or "nothingness" bother us. But when we jump into that special pond we call shunyata, words don't bother us. Slay. Slay!

Usually, we miss the last sentence of this excerpt: "By not clinging to things, you freely pass through."

Everybody wants to "freely pass through" but everybody does a lot of clinging to things. We have fears, and innumerable attachments. Dogen Zenji's style of saying this same thing is this way: "When you have cast off body and mind and entered the realm of Buddha, he will lead you. If you follow his Way, you achieve detachment from life and death, and without effort or using your mind, become Buddha."

When you cast off body and mind — slay, slay — Dharma will take care of it. You achieve detachment.

So don't just think, "Oh, this is one of those interesting stories about Rinzai."

Slay! Slay! Mu! Mu! There is no other way.

•

Independence Day

Text: Rinzai Roku, Discourses XVIII

> Among all the students from every quarter who are Followers of the Way, none has yet come before me without being dependent on something. Here I hit them right from the start. If they come forth using their hands, I hit them at the hands; if they come forth using their mouths, I hit them at the mouth; if they come forth using their eyes, I hit them at the eyes. Not one has yet come before me in solitary freedom. All are clambering after the worthless contrivances of the men of old.
> As for myself, I haven't a single dharma to give to them. All I can do is cure illnesses and loosen bonds.
> You Followers of the Way from every quarter, try coming before me without being dependent upon things.
> Five years, nay ten years, have passed but as yet not one *person* has appeared. All have been ghosts, dependent upon grasses or attached to leaves, souls of bamboos and trees, wild fox spirits. They recklessly gnaw on all kinds of dung clods. Blind fools! Wastefully squandering the alms given them by believers everywhere and saying, "I am a renouncer of home" all the while holding such views as these!

This section of the Rinzai Roku is very deep.

Not one person has come before Rinzai without being dependent on something. When we look at ourselves — never mind the students of Rinzai Gigen Zenji in China — we see that we depend either on the sangha's support, or the zendo-leader's encouragement, or sutra-chanting, or koan studies, or on breath-counting, or on you-name-it.

Reading this sentence of the text very carefully, we come to understand that Master Rinzai was quite strict in one sense, extremely idealistic in another sense, and purist in yet another sense. He denies us all the things we count on.

"Here I hit them" — I deprive, I snatch away from them — "right from the start." That expression is *very* good: right from the beginning.

"If they come forth using their hands, I hit them at the hands" — but let's read this carefully. You *may* use a hand to express this inexpressible matter. But Master Hakuin's use of the hand to answer the question, "What is the sound of one hand clapping?" or Gutei's use of "One Finger" — these uses of the hand are, so to speak, copyrighted. If *you* used them, Rinzai would "hit" you at the hand — deprive you of your imitative hand-expression.

"If they come forth using their mouths, I hit them at the mouth." Even closing the mouth is using the mouth! He would "deprive" you — a better word than "hit" — of the use of the mouth.

"Not *one* has yet come before me in solitary freedom." He means free from the body, free from Buddha, free from Dharma, free from zazen, free from sutras, free from Mu! "All are clambering after the worthless contrivances of the men of old."

This is very severe. We use Hakuin's koan system; we use the Gateless Gate, the Platform Sutra, and other "worthless contrivances". Rinzai could have used Obaku's Denshin Hoyo, or the Sixth Patriarch's Platform Sutra, or the Third Patriarch's Believing in Mind. But to him, none of these had a fresh, vital dynamism. They were just commentary or explanation. He didn't use any text for a discourse the way we are using the Rinzai Roku on this day of sesshin. He spoke without depending on any text, on any ancient Dharma dialogues or old happenings. But nowadays we depend on *so* many things: Zen texts, Zen rules, sesshins, koans, zazen, sutras. So Rinzai was a romanticist or idealist, and a purist. "All are clambering after the worthless contrivances of the men of old." Strictly speaking — *strictly* speaking — Mu alone is enough. And without even Mu, and without depending on zazen, true insight is enough. It's all we need.

"As for myself, I haven't a single dharma to give to you."

Why? *Because* you are as you are and cannot be otherwise. In other words, you are — *as* you are — "Buddha". And cannot be otherwise.

Many of you say, "Well, I, Buddha? That's hard to believe."

You don't have enough faith, therefore you cannot become Buddha. Rinzai says, "You don't have enough faith."

Let me read this to you.

> "Do you know where the disease lies which keeps you students from reaching true insight? It lies where you have no faith in yourself. When faith in yourself is lacking, you find yourself harried by others in every possible way. At every encounter, you are no longer your own master. You are driven about by others, this way and that."

Isn't this quite true?

"As for myself, I haven't a single dharma to give to you" means you already have it. You already are Buddha regardless of appearance or age, for instance. But many of us think, "Oh, I am so imperfect. I am imperfect. If I become perfect, I can accept that." That's how our bumpkin logic goes. According to Rinzai, that's the very reason you cannot, as we say, "get it".

"All I can do is cure illness and loosen bonds. Come before me without being dependent upon things" and we would meet in a really true encounter. We would enter the realm of Mu.

Dependent ghosts. "Blind fools! Wastefully squandering the alms given them by believers everywhere and yet saying, 'I am a renouncer of home'."

If you have a copy of the Rinzai Roku, read that part ten or twenty times.

Master Rinzai used the expression, "True man without rank."

True man without rank, without zazen, without koan, without zendo, without sesshin — truly *free*. Free from all the stuff we think is precious. Even to say "a woman of Zen" or "a Zen man" is binding. This is Rinzai, the purist. Not being a dependent ghost — that's ideal. But realistically we need the sangha to support each other; we need the monastery to congregate in; we need sesshin to help us make changes in ourselves; we need zazen to practice concentration, among many other reasons; all these things we need, need, need. I want, I want, I want.

Some of it cannot be helped, but we must minimize the needs.

•

Can You "Do Nothing"?

Text: Rinzai Roku, Discourses XVIII

> I say to you there is no Buddha, no Dharma, nothing to practice, nothing to prove. Just what are you seeking thus in the highways and byways? Blind fool! You are putting a head on top of the one you already have. What do you yourself lack? Followers of the Way, your own present activities do not differ from those of the patriarch-buddhas. You just don't believe this and keep on seeking outside. Make no mistake! Outside, there is no Dharma; inside, there is none to be obtained. Rather than grasping at the words from my mouth, take it easy and do nothing.

In other passages, Rinzai gives us encouragement and pushes us to do what we must *do*. We must study. We must slay the Buddha. Generally during sesshin we emphasize these things. Zazen is very important. Concentration is essential. Discipline: don't look around, be quiet in your actions, and so on. Many of you still resist but this is why sesshin follows a hard schedule.

But in today's text, Rinzai speaks in a completely different way. He speaks from shunyata. From his realization. We recite, "When I, a student of Dharma, look at the real form of the universe, all is the never-failing manifestation of the mysterious truth of shunyata (we usually say *Tathagata* but the meaning here is the same). In any event, in any place, and in any moment, all is the marvelous revelation of shunyata's glorious light." It is from *this* point of view that he is now talking. Remember there are two different kinds of teaching: one, encouragement; two, direct pointing. This text is more than encouragement; it is true teisho.

"I say to you there is no Buddha, no Dharma, nothing to practice, nothing to prove."

When we hear this kind of sentence we are either confused, or we find it a good excuse not to study and practice. But, in truth, there are two different levels of speaking. On the shallower level we say, sit hard, don't move, do Mu — and these things are necessary. On the deeper level, actually right *here,* the formless, nameless, ageless, rankless, positionless someone, temporarily called Rinzai Gigen, says there is no Buddha as such, no Dharma as such, no practice as such.

Rinzai asks, "Just what are you seeking in the highways and byways? Blind fool! You are putting a head on top of the one you already have."

We recite, "We are like the son of a rich man who wandered away among the poor. We are like a man who, in the midst of water, cries in thirst so imploringly." We want, we want, still we cannot have enough. Somehow, we think we have to make progress. We want progress. But true progress is to realize that we are like the son of a rich man. We already are in the midst of water so there's no need to cry in thirst so imploringly. To realize *this* is true progress.

Nyogen Senzaki, in his last words, said: "Don't put a false head above your own." He departed on May 6th, 1958. This kind of speaking is real teisho.

Let's try to imagine someone who *doesn't* want longevity, good health, happiness, wealth.

The person who doesn't want these things is very brave and very strong. That person has truly realized that "wanting" is putting another head above your own. You are already fulfilled. This you must believe. You may say "more money" but you don't know the suffering of having money. Once I was a millionaire so I know the suffering of money, but now I know that when we continue this practice, the money comes all by itself. And goes all by itself! But somehow there will always be sufficient to survive. That's why I always remind you about the three Ds: Do your best; Don't worry; Dharma will take care of it.

"What do you yourself lack?"

You often hear Zen Buddhists say, "Everything is perfect." Or, "Things are as they are, perfect, and cannot be otherwise." Usually we regard perfection as an ideal. But here we look at things in a slightly different way — in fact, in a completely different way. Someone catches a cold. A temporary phenomenon. At *that* moment, he is perfect as he is. This is so hard to believe. It is so hard to be contented. I need this and I need that. I regret this and that. I hope in the future this will happen. I wish I were...and so on and so forth. Right? And what do you have? In one word, may I say, frustration. And we repeat this and we are repeatedly frustrated. And repeatedly we dream, and repeatedly we are frustrated, instead of: I am what I am right now; I am what I am. I am penniless right now. It doesn't mean I will be penniless tomorrow. Who knows?

This different way of thinking is very, very difficult for our civilization, very difficult to accept. But I think the time has come for us to change our attitude instead of being frustrated and constantly complaining. At least from time to time try to be contented and grateful, and then the world will be changed. And you know, positive vibrations attract, like magnetism. Negative vibrations cause things somehow to run away. So you are missing a good opportunity in this great contradiction: the more you want, the more it goes; the less you want, the more it comes. I don't know why, but somehow it works that way.

"What do you yourself lack? Followers of the Way, your own present activities do not differ from those of the patriarch-buddhas."

We have a tendency to think: Shakyamuni Buddha is impeccable; Bodhidharma is very close to impeccability; Rinzai sounds impeccable; Hakuin seems impeccable. We idealize buddhas and patriarchs and sages. And then when we look at ourselves, it's hard for us to say, "I am impeccable." I am peccable! But Shakyamuni Buddha sneezed when he had a cold. Bodhidharma didn't sit for nine years — he stood up and sat down; he ate and went to the bathroom; at night he slept.

"Followers of the Way, your own present activities do not differ from those of the patriarch-buddhas. You just don't believe this and keep on seeking outside. Make no mistake! Outside there is no Dharma. Inside, there is none to be obtained."

In fact, there is nothing. There is no outside as such, no inside as such, no between as such. In fact, this cannot be talked about. But nevertheless we talk about it in several different ways, such as "shunyata", or more positively, "One Mind", or more mysteriously, "Mu".

"Rather than grasping at the words from my mouth, take it easy and *do* nothing."

Now this is very important: intonation. Don't read: "Take-it-easy-and-do-nothing." *Take* — *take!* it easy and *DO* nothing. This is a very great koan. Can you do nothing? If you stand up, you are standing. If you are sitting, people may say you are sitting, doing nothing. No, you are sitting. *Do* nothing. This is one of the key terms in the Rinzai Roku.

D. T. Suzuki has written a very comprehensible and intelligent explanation of this "bu-ji", this "do nothing". I'll read it to you.

> "Bu-ji" is one of the most significant terms in the vocabulary of Zen, especially in the Rinzai School. The term, however, is liable to be grossly misinterpreted by those who are not used to the Oriental way of living and feeling. When the Dharma is truly, fully, experientially understood, we find that there is nothing wanting in this life as we live it. Everything and anything we need is here with us, and in us. One who has actually experienced this is called 'a man of bu-ji'. Bu-ji is one of those concepts whose equivalent probably cannot be found in any European language because in the thought structure of the West, there is nothing corresponding to it. The words 'non-action' or 'not-doing' may be all right for Laotsu's 'mu-i'. 'No-mind' may do for Eno Daikan's 'Mu-shin'. But 'no-business' or 'no-event' is very misleading for Rinzai's 'bu-ji'. The trouble with bu-ji is that

there is no good word in English expressing all the ideas implied in 'ji'. Ji generally means event, business, matter, concern, engagement, affair, etcetera. When all this is negated by 'bu', we may have for a man of bu-ji one who has no business, or one to whom no events happen, or one who is unconcerned or indifferent, or disinterested, or one to whom nothing matters, and so on. But a man of bu-ji is not any of these. He is one who has a true understanding of Dharma, or the reality of the universe. He is one who, being freed from the externalities of matter *is* a Buddha and patriarch. He has the great business of trying to lead all his fellow beings into a state of enlightenment. He cannot remain unconcerned and indifferent so long as there is even one being left unemancipated. He works hard. As Zen people would say, he is really one of the busiest men of the world. And yet, he does no business; no events are happening to him. He is utterly unconcerned. What kind of man can he be? One of the aristocracy, to use Eckhardtian terminology. Zen calls him a man of bu-ji.

"Take it easy and do nothing." Previously Rinzai said, "Hard work, grinding discipline, exhaustive investigation." But here he says, "Take it easy and do nothing."

It's not at all easy.

•

Leaving the Cage

Text: Rinzai Roku, Critical Examinations XXIV

One day, Fuke went about the streets asking people he met for a one-piece robe. They all offered him one, but Fuke declined them all. Rinzai had the steward of the temple buy a coffin, and when Fuke came the Master said, "I've made a one-piece robe for you." Fuke put the coffin on his shoulders and went around the streets calling out, "Rinzai made me a one-piece robe. I'm going to the East Gate to depart this life." All the townspeople scrambled after him to watch. "No, not today," said Fuke, "but tomorrow I'll go to the South Gate to depart this life." After he had said the same thing for three days, no one believed him any more. On the fourth day, not a single person followed him to watch. He went outside the town walls all by himself, got into the coffin, and asked a passerby to nail it down. The news immediately got about. The townspeople all came running. On opening the coffin, they saw he had vanished, body and all. Only the sound of his bell could be heard in the sky, receding, chjing...chjing...chjing.... ..

This person Fuke is a lunatic. I will explain in a minute.

Fuke (pronounced Fu-kay) is said to be the Dharma heir of Banzan Hoshaku Zenji, and *he* was the heir of Baso Do Itsu Zenji. In the lineage we recite, Hyakujo comes after Baso, but Baso had many Dharma heirs. One of them was Banzan.

There's an interesting story about Banzan Hoshaku Zenji. Once, he was walking on the street and there was a butcher shop. For some reason, he wanted to buy some meat.

He asked, "Is it fresh?"

The butcher said, "You cannot find anything here that is not fresh."

In other words, everything is fresh. Everything is, as we say, Mu!

Hearing this, in front of the butcher shop, Banzan gained clear insight.

Now Fuke plays an interesting Dharma role. You can find such a person in your own life. Fuke was already at the temple to which Rinzai finally came. He was already there to assist. And then when Rinzai had become established as a teacher, Fuke disappeared. You must know one or two individuals in your own life who seemed to be there in order to assist you in your work, and then when your work was really progressing, these people disappeared. We have had many Fukes, and not all were "lunatics". When we truly understand Dharma, we understand these mysterious happenings and we don't ignore them. Instead we appreciate them. You too are brief Fukes. Without you, we could not do this wonderful sesshin. But sooner or later you will be disappearing, and in the meantime another Fuke will join and the tradition will be carried on and on.

But this particular Fuke was more than "far out". To explain this, I need to explain some misunderstandings, especially about the purpose of zazen practice.

There is a Japanese word: *kyogai*. It isn't in English dictionaries. I'm talking now about Fuke's kyogai. It is a state of mind, or way of living, in the most free, most detached, most unsticky way, transcending common sense, right and wrong, or what is proper and improper.

We are in a cage, like a bird, and the cage says, "Inside is safe. Outside may be dangerous. So you must not go out. You must stay in." And we're afraid, therefore we stay in the cage while longing for real freedom. Having kyogai means a person has a brave and clear understanding about This Matter and is not afraid to leave the cage. What he or she does looks very strange; it's not in the category of common sense. What is said is incomprehensible. Gempo Roshi had a special kyogai. The danger is that some people, without having a breakthrough into profound experience, simply imitate this behavior.

To introduce Fuke, here are some stories from the Rinzai Roku.

One day, when Master Rinzai and the venerable priests Kaiyo and Mokuto were sitting together around the fire-pit in the monks' hall, Rinzai said, "Every day Fuke goes through the streets acting like a lunatic. Who knows whether he is a commoner or a sage?"

Before he had finished speaking, Fuke came in and joined them. "Are you a commoner or a sage?" Rinzai asked.

"Now you tell me whether I'm a commoner or a sage," answered Fuke.

Rinzai shouted.

Pointing his finger at them, Fuke said, "Kaiyo is a new bride. Mokuto is a Zen granny, and Rinzai is a snotty child but he has the Dharma Eye."

"You thief!" cried the Master.

"Thief, thief," cried Fuke and went out.

Another story: One day, Fuke was eating raw vegetables in front of the monks' hall. The master saw him and said, "Just like an ass!"

"Hee haw! Hee haw!" brayed Fuke.

"You thief!" said the Master.

"Thief, thief!" cried Fuke, and went off.

A few comments are necessary. We have an expression in Japanese: "I don't understand whether he is clever or a fool." He is so incomprehensible. Is he stupid or is he bright? This is the same thing as, "Are you a commoner or a sage?" What we have to learn — this is a very subtle point of zazen practice — is to become a person who cannot be labeled by others as stupid or brilliant.

Once in a great while we find a person we cannot categorize. That person is ungraspable, incomprehensible. "What is he or she thinking about? What is the intention?" That's called kyogai. Most of us have a fixed label: "I am sharp" — like T-shirts — I am cute, I am such-and-such. But a plain, plain T-shirt is really saying, "Are you a commoner or a sage?"

"Thief, thief!" appears twice. In another place, Master Rinzai says, "I have nothing to give you." This is a very profound. He is saying, "I have nothing to give you: no Dharma to give you; no discipline to give you; nothing to give you. All I do is deprive, snatch, take away whatever you have." And we have a lot. We have some measure of material things. But we have a great deal of mental, emotional, and psychological stuff. So Rinzai, the thief, deprives you. He takes away, snatches! steals — to make each one of you naked, mentally naked, psychologically naked, emotionally naked so that, for instance, you have no anger.

Read the Rinzai Roku again and again. I can't find any Christians who are not familiar with the Bible, especially the New Testament. But there are plenty of Zen students who have never read the Rinzai Roku. What's the matter? My mother attended a Rinzai temple and I'm positively sure she never read the Rinzai Roku. Why?!

Fuke was always going around the streets ringing a little bell. He called out, "Coming as brightness, I *hit* the brightness. Coming as darkness, I hit the darkness. Coming from the four quarters and eight directions, I hit like a whirlwind. Coming from empty sky, I lash like a flail."

Master Rinzai told his attendant that the moment he heard Fuke say these words, he must grab him and ask, "If coming is not at all thus, what then?"

The attendant did this. Fuke pushed him away saying, "There will be a feast tomorrow at Daihi-in Temple." The attendant returned and told this to Master Rinzai.

The Master said, "I've always held wonder for that fellow."

Here is some explanation of "coming as brightness, I hit as brightness." In the Lotus Sutra there is a section that can be translated like this: "The Buddha replied to the Bodhisattva Infinite Thought, 'Good son, if the living in any realm must be saved in the body of the Buddha, the Bodhisattva Regarder of the Cries of the World'" — that is, Kanzeon, or Kannon — " 'appears as a Buddha and preaches to them the Law. To those who must be saved in the body of the Pratyeka Buddha, he appears as Pratyeka Buddha and preaches to them the Law.'"

To those who must be emancipated in the body of a bus-driver, he appears as a bus-driver and preaches the Dharma. He appears as a bank-teller and preaches the Dharma. He appears as a graphic artist and preaches the Dharma.

So, "Coming as brightness, I hit the brightness; coming as darkness, I hit the darkness."

"One day, Fuke went about the streets asking people he met for a one-piece robe. They all offered him one."

If he were really crazy, if he did not truly help Rinzai's Buddhadharma, perhaps people wouldn't even hear him. But they all knew what Fuke did for the Dharma so, delightedly, they all offered him one.

"But Fuke declined them all.

Rinzai asked a steward of the temple to buy a coffin and when Fuke came back, the Master said, 'I have made a one-piece robe for you.' Upon seeing it, Fuke was so delighted that he put the coffin on his shoulders and went around the street calling out, 'Rinzai made me a one-piece robe. I'm going to the East Gate to depart this life.'"

When Gempo Roshi was ninety-six years old, he began saying, "I would like to finish my comedian life."

Maybe this is difficult for you to understand, but he considered this world a comedy. Crying, shouting, eating, being serious — it's comedy. The problem is, we don't think this way. We don't *want* to think this is a comedy. "This is serious!" But it's a comedy.

So Gempo Roshi said that he would like to conclude his comedy and say goodby to the comedian world. His attendant monk said, "Roshi, if you die now, it's a very bad time because the farmers are planting rice and it's a very busy time to hold a funeral service. Can you postpone it?" And he said, "All right, I'll postpone it."

He died on June 4, 1961.

The point is, Gempo Roshi had his own kyogai. He was free to postpone departing, and free to depart, this life. It's easy to say,

"I'll leave this place tomorrow, or I'll postpone leaving until Friday." But leaving from this world is not so easy. We still think that death is something that's not good, that's unhappy, miserable, and fearful because it's a different realm. Even though this life is full of pain, still we have lots of attachment to it. We're not so free, coming and going; our kyogai is not well cultivated. But in Gempo Roshi's case, and in Fuke's case, "I will depart tomorrow." How many of us can say, "I will depart this world this afternoon?"

So the key point of this strange story of Fuke is that it shows the real meaning of freedom from birth-and-death.

All the townspeople ran after him to watch — this is quite understandable. Naturally they were curious.

"Ah no, not today," said Fuke. This is wonderful. Oh no, not *today*. But *tomorrow* I will go to the South Gate to depart this life. And fewer scrambled after him.

And after he had said the same thing for three days, no one believed him any more. From a commonsense viewpoint, this is quite understandable.

"On the fourth day, not a single person followed him to watch. So he carried his coffin outside the town wall all by himself, got into the coffin and asked a passerby — evidently someone passed by so, "Wait a minute, would you be good enough to nail...?" — and he did.

The news immediately got about. The townspeople came running and someone suggested the coffin be opened. "This is an important person; we must have a funeral."

The next sentence is very good: "They saw he had vanished, body and all."

In this way, the Rinzai Roku speaks of shunyata. In this dramatic and poetic way, the Rinzai Roku speaks of self-lessness, body-lessness. They saw he had vanished, body and all.

Only the receding sound of his bell could be heard in the sky, chjing...chjing...chjing....

•

Appendix

Addresses

The Zen Studies Society

Dai Bosatsu Zendo
HCR 1, Box 171
Livingston Manor, New York 12758
914-439-4566

New York Zendo
223 East 67th Street
New York, New York 10021
212-861-3333

Affiliates

Kashin Zendo Genzo-ji
Jiro Andy Afable Sensei, Director
7004 Ninth Street, NW
Washington, DC 20012
202-829-1966

Ginzan Sangha
Koun John Burden, Director
3060 Sagittarius Drive
Reno, Nevada 89509
702-786-1484

Kanzeon Zen Yoga Center
25 Deer Run
Corte Madera, California 94925
415-924-5322

Rinzai Zen Gesselshaft in der Schweiz
Regensbergstrasse 80
CH-8050 Zürich
Switzerland

•

Interior Design and Typography:
Dianne Borneman, Shadow Canyon Graphics, Evergreen, CO

Cover Design and Typography:
Dianne Borneman, Shadow Canyon Graphics, Evergreen, CO

Printed on recycled, acid-free paper by:
Thomson-Shore, Dexter, MI